MORE THAN OUR JOBS

MORE THAN OUR JOBS
An Anthology

Edited by
GLEN DOWNIE
and
PAM TRANFIELD

PULP
PRESS

Vancouver

Published by
PULP PRESS BOOK PUBLISHERS
Arsenal Pulp Press Ltd.
100-1062 Homer Street
Vancouver, B.C. V6B 2W9
Canada

COVER PHOTO: Vancouver boot factory, 1923. Courtesy of Vancouver Public Library
INTERIOR PHOTOS: B.C. Marine Shipbuilders, Vancouver, 1975-76. David R. Conn
SKETCHES: Phil Hall
PRINTING: Hignell Printing
TYPESETTING: Vancouver Desktop Publishing Centre
PRINTED AND BOUND IN CANADA

CANADIAN CATALOGUING IN PUBLICATION DATA:
Main entry under title:
More than our jobs.

ISBN 0-88978-231-8

1. Canadian literature (English)—20th century.* 2. Working class writings, Canadian. 3. Work—Literary collections.
I. Downie, Glen, 1953– II. Tranfield, Pam, 1960–
PS8235.W73M67 1991   C810.8'090623
PR9194.5.W73M67 1991   C91-091139-8

CONTENTS

INTRODUCTION

On buses and in art galleries, in churches and in coffee houses, in the open air of the Folk Festival and the quiet of local bookstores; from hand to hand in books and broadsheets, from mouth to ear on the airwaves and cassette, the Vancouver Industrial Writers Union's unique brand of literature is steadily getting around.

It has been more than five years since the publication of *Shop Talk*, the first anthology by VIWU, and over ten years since the group itself was formed. Through the years, VIWU has been stretched and challenged by the growth of its members, and while individuals leave and new ones join, the group itself seems to grow and strengthen and thrive. For some of our audience, VIWU has become a fixture on the literary scene; yet with each performance in a non-literary venue, we meet more people for whom VIWU and the idea of work literature is a new and exciting notion. Our collaborations with our folk music colleagues, Fraser Union, have not only brought poetry and song together in lively interaction on the cassette *Split Shift*, but have convinced still more people of the relevance poetry can have to their lives.

As this continued energy fostered the writing of more material and attracted new voices, another anthology became inevitable. As the title suggests, we have taken the opportunity to flesh out the group's self-portrait. Work, we remind our readers, has never been our exclusive interest, nor poetry our only form. Our members have written fiction, drama, essays, and criticism, and tried their hands at radio documentary and labour history; there are even a couple of novels in the works. This anthology reflects some of that diversity. And while we have no intention of abandoning the writing that comes from the workplace—that place Mark Warrior calls the fulcrum of our life— we also hope that our writing will reflect the wider personal and social context in which the dramas of working life take place. In linking the sections of overtly 'work' writing to others which focus on our ties to community, lovers, and family, we urge not a narrow view of ourselves and our world but a broad one. For, as Charlie King's song says, "Our life is more than our work/And our work is more than our jobs."

—G.D. for VIWU

Initiation

KIRSTEN EMMOTT

Shamanic Journey

> "Transpersonal crises of this type bear a deep resemblance to what the anthropologists have described as the *shamanic* or *initiatory* illness (Eliade, 1964). It is a dramatic episode of a nonordinary state of consciousness that marks the beginning of the career of many shamans."
> —Christina and Stanislav Grof
> *Spiritual Emergency: the Understanding and Treatment of Transpersonal Crises*

The core experience of the shamanic journey is a profound encounter with death and subsequent rebirth.

Yes, I have encountered these. On the very first day of medical school we were escorted to the hospital, met on the wide stairs by an elder, taken to the halls of birth and death, saw a baby born, and then the morgue.

Initiatory dreams and visions include a descent into the underworld

During that first year we went every day behind the door marked "Authorized Personnel Only." Gross Lab was a private morgue for the sixty of us. Most of us had never seen death before. We were to follow it down every twist and turn it took, shred it into so many small pieces that we would lose our fears of it.

under the guidance of ancestral spirits,

Our teachers knew where the nerves and arteries lay buried. They warned us to have respect for the corpses, to study hard, and not to leave skulls on the bus.

attacked by demons,

No, not the easily enraged surgeons, nor the violent drunks in Emergency, nor the germs they carried, but our terrors, which we had to keep buried.

exposure to unimaginable emotional and physical tortures,

There was no sleep. Few meals. Internship was a year but residency was years more. Blood splashed on your shoes. People began to scream when you told them their dear one had just died.

and finally complete annihilation.

There comes a time when you know if you get one more call tonight, you will scream and pound the bedside table where the relentless phone sits and then go, stumbling with weariness, completely blank except for the little bit that remembers how to do a cardiogram or a forceps delivery.

This is then typically followed by sequences of rebirth

The babies never failed to bring it back. For those few minutes between the sight of the head, and the paperwork after, I was alive.

and ascent to supernal realms.

You can see the interns occasionally, standing at a window staring out over the city just before dawn, no longer able to think, but still able to feel, wondering what comes next.

Although there exist considerable variations in the details of these ordeals among different tribes

When I was a resident it was no better, although the rewards came more quickly; many more babies, much more abuse.

and individual shamans

There were a dozen of us and many did not notice anything odd about the way we were living, for in spirit they were still in the Gross Lab where the wishes of the "subjects" no longer existed.

they all share the general atmosphere

There was a single on-call room, but there was a screen, which I could go behind to express the milk that I could no longer give my baby; the other residents would turn on their heels and walk out when they saw me.

of horror and inhuman suffering.

We were as kind as we knew how. This was not enough. There was death now and then, and considerable pain for the patients. We tried to care about them. Nobody cared about us, not even ourselves.

The tortures involve experiences of dismemberment,

Dismemberment. What are your members? Is your uterus a member of you? Do you need crutches to walk with only one ovary?

disposal of all body fluids,

blood, amniotic fluid, shit. Tears. More blood. More tears; ours.

scraping of flesh from bones,

When scraping out the uterus lining with a curette, wait for the gritty sensation of metal against myometrial muscle. It makes the sound you would expect.

tearing eyes from the sockets,

We did that, yes, but the eyes are ovarian cysts and we delighted in our skill at shelling them out neatly. And fibroids. Neatly.

or similar terrifying manipulations.

No one was being tortured; the babies were born, the women operated on while in a deep sleep, the doctors were learning, all night.

After the novice shaman has been reduced to a skeleton

I had forgotten the ideas I had come into the program with. I was disappointed at not becoming a surgeon; I would not be permitted to become easily enraged.

the bones are covered with new flesh

I became a G.P. I took out a bank loan, I bought a desk. Fish tanks, baby fish.

and he or she receives fresh blood.

Women came to see me, asking for my hands. Men and babies and old people came in my door, they sat down and talked about themselves, they wanted me to know.

The next important stage of the shamanic journey is the ascent to the heavenly regions

The day came when I delivered Jane, and signed my name to the chart, the reward of having managed it, done it, finished it:

by means of a pole, birch tree, rainbow, or a magical flight.

There is an elevator to the fifth floor that only Staff can use. If you know the right button to push, the back door opens right into the delivery suite.

In a genuine shaman, the initiatory death is always followed by resurrection

It is born. I am born. We are born.

resolution of the crisis

This does not happen. There is an endless flow of interesting work to do. There is always a crisis but it no longer lurks behind a door marked for personnel more authorized than I.

and good integration of the experience into everyday life. Accomplished shamans have to be able to function in the ordinary world as well as or better than their fellow tribesmen.

They are not expected to stand looking out that window and thinking, but to remain active, showing neither cruelty nor pity. They are not to become demoralized.

They are good businessmen

If you have no intention of paying for our services, kindly announce this at the first interview.

practical psychologists,

There is no end to the griefs that people bring us; there is, however, an end to the working day. When we meet you on the street, we have forgotten all those secrets you told us, believe me.

masters of ceremonies,

Ceremonies I know, exulting in my secret heart as the baby is born, even as I remain smooth-browed. I know how to put the child in the father's arms. I know how to lead the relatives in to say goodbye to the corpse. I applaud the marriage, I arrange the adoption with joyful hello on one hand and sad goodbye on the other.

artists and poets, as well as healers, seers, and psychopomps.

I brought an artist to sketch the labours. She is a poet too. As for being a healer and seer, surely I can diagnose some ailments over the telephone. From listening to the spouse. From weighing the child.

They feel at home in the ordinary and nonordinary realities, can cross their threshholds at will, and are able to mediate this transition for other people.

I tell the tense businessman to meditate, the pregnant lawyer to learn Lamaze breathing. I tell the New Age mother that herbs will not protect her child from polio, that there are no nerves to the legs that can be affected by manipulating the cranium. I show poetry to surgeons and immunology texts to theosophists.

In the experiences of individuals whose transpersonal crises have strong shamanic features, there is great emphasis on personal suffering and encounter with death followed by rebirth and elements of ascent or magical flight.

I have not suffered as these poor people have suffered. For me there was no abandonment, no widowhood, no beatings, no rape, no stillbirth, no death. All these encounters I watched happen to others. They are there in my soul just the same. I needed the rebirth; every descent into the maelstrom of other people's lives requires that I ascend again into my own. At night I dream, not of flying, but of perfect births.

They also typically sense a special connection with the elements of nature

My office is filled with plants. I have no patience with wistful beliefs that plants think, hear, know us. They grow, that is enough.

and experience communication with animals or animal spirits.

Tropical fish. They grow, they reproduce. Are well known to have a calming effect on distraught people. I put the tanks on the filing cabinets. They swim regally over the facts.

it is also not unusual to feel an upsurge of extraordinary powers and impulses to heal.

It is you who have given me this; the extraordinary powers were yours. I have taken what happened to you and made it part of myself. The struggle ahead is learning how to give some of it back.

GLEN DOWNIE

Living with Cancer

The new patient is appalled at the gallows
humour before the meeting starts.
Loose talk about death

has spooked him, driven him
to the edge

of our circle, where he whispers to his wife
about leaving early.

Newly hired, I'm here to observe the human
chemistry, as the group administers a dose
of distilled experience.
Cancer is alive in the room, yet the laughing presence

of 10- and 12-year veterans
confounds the man's fear.

When I started work, someone issued me
a daybook. Religiously, I snip
a corner off each clean page

to be always in the present, to feel the edge
of the cut day against my thumb, and know I am right
where I belong.
                    Tomorrow, we will spread
out in a bigger building, my office
one cell in a growing cancer

clinic. Like the stranger tonight, I'm new
to this disease, but as a comfort
the old hands assure me
we will soon be
well acquainted.

PAM TRANFIELD

Death Benefits

a new job   a new desk
my first task   to remove
the former occupant's tools;

her name is on everything,
in scroll above the floral design
on an unwashed coffee cup
underlined on the cover
of a speller's dictionary   and
in dot matrix
on a bottle of white pills:
Mary R.

Miss Q.
hums along to her computer terminal,
a drone
she smells of fine old cheese   sweats
cigarette smoke
eats french fries at morning coffee.

we both have benefitted
from Mary R.'s death;
I got off UIC
into Mary's desk,
Miss Q.
got Mary's position   wages
computer;
under her fingers
the terminal keys respond
clatter like a rosary on this
her wedding day;
Miss Q. and The Government
till death do you part.

KATE BRAID

Excerpts from
The Radio Documentary

January 26, 1990

What am I doing here? At our first "production" meeting (what is "production"?) Don, the producer, gives me two documentaries to take home, listen to. One is about Tolstoy, the other about a woman with whom he produced twelve documentaries for radio, eleven of which won awards. The entire time she had cancer and this is her story. As I listen I try to pay attention to technique—how did he do this, not just what—but my ear feels thick with rust. ("Listen," he has been saying to me since I first wrote the letter. "Listen!")

But all I know is that both documentaries move me, are beautiful in content and also for how the music plays like another voice, speaking in another language.

I am inspired and the terror only sets in slowly. Who am I to think that I, too, can do this? I'm only a carpenter who likes the sounds of women talking about their work as welders, electricians, boiler-makers. I know two-by-fours, lumber and nails, physical things. How do you put your hands on a sound? In tears I telephone, "I can't. I don't know how. There's no time to learn a new trade."

"Don't worry," Don says, over and over. I think he has taken assertiveness training. He repeats himself until I hear it. "Don't worry." Monday morning we will begin. When I think about it, I start to cry again. I feel bare, sterile. There is nothing in me that sees beyond the twelve precious tapes I carry from my travels, twelve voices talking about their trades, about being women, about being men working with women. All the richness is in them and I am the stone wall they are scratched upon. Not a single blade of grass grows here.

January 29, 1990

Monday. He sits me in an airless room, padded so all sound dies before it passes the door. In front of us is a small steel stand on which sit two innocent, empty reels. I know this word, "reels." I don't know what he means when he says, "Edit." I wait.

He turns it on. "Who do we want first?" he asks. I swallow panic. "How should I know?" I want to cry. Instead, I blurt the first name that comes to mind. He nods, as if I have said something intelligent, and threads a tape on the reel.

Then he shows me how to edit.

You play the tape until you find the piece you want. Stop. Mark the exact spot with a yellow wax crayon, this one with the string hanging off the side, the kind my mother used to mark her canned peaches, a humble grease marker, antique device.

Now he lifts the tape off the reel, pulling slowly, lays it in a small steel bed I hadn't noticed before, below the reels. Following the groove in the steel, he cuts the tape with a razor blade like the one I use to clean my windows.

By hand? This technique is practically medieval. By hand?

My question is lost in the padded walls before it reaches the door. "It will match the next cut," he says as if he was speaking before. Did he speak? "Now we stick them together." He is concentrating now, all his attention on the dark brown tape glistening like slough water in the thin steel trough. He slides a second piece up to meet it, a perfect match, then takes a one inch strip of translucent tape off a roll like the one on any desk, only narrower. He lays the tape in the metal channel over the two matching pieces, careful, then rubs vigorously with a short forefinger to improve the connection. Tape, I think. Scotch tape! Is this professional?

But already he is lifting my tapes from the box to show me another. Get it? But it's so labour intensive, like . . . .

Like the methodical joining of board to board until one day you look up and you have created a house. I couldn't believe that at first, either, that it wasn't magic but so much common sense and skill and repetition. There was more, much more, later, but I remember how it struck me as simple at first. One piece at a time. Cut and nail. Almost disappointed, then relieved that even I could do this, cut and nail, slowly building toward a roofline, a window, a door. Only later would I find there was magic, after all.

I look up in recognition of that other building process but Don mistakes it for acknowledgement of this one. "I can figure it out," I say. "Where's the magic?"

"It comes later," he says.

February 2, 1990

We discuss the question of music and sounds. I am on quicksand again. Don is intrigued by the fact that Heather, the boilermaker, says a boiler, when she is inside repairing it, sounds like "a great wild thing" and later, " like a pipe organ." He ignores my furrowed brow and presses me about the sounds of a boiler.

I am a carpenter. I avoid metal things. I have no idea what a boiler sounds like in any state. Great. That makes two of us.

I travel around the city recording sounds—welding sounds, Rapid Transit sounds, carpentry and machining and finally the boiler. A boiler is a great empty can. The teacher at the trade school plainly thinks I am mad when, in desperation, I crawl inside one of these rusted monsters and record silence, then ask students to beat on the outside. But no one is happy. These are the sounds of an empty tin can, not a wild thing.

As I leave, I pass a huge cannister that has something to do with the vacuum system. It is humming steadily, almost like a living thing. Grimly I record it in passing, better than the thin things I have so far.

❖

February 10, 1990

Perhaps he is not a radio producer at all but a tinsmith. What has he done to the rust in my ears? Tonight I take out the Tolstoy and the cancer tapes, listen again and now I hear something new.

❖

He makes leaps that logic would never dare and I am grateful. This is part of it, then, to move from one voice to another, not as I would think but as I feel.

February 14, 1990

Every step in this process is a sort of miracle to me. Who was the disciple who watched Jesus walk on water and wanted to do that too?

I stepped into radio because Don said "Walk!" And where there appeared to be nothing, no ground but black water, I am suddenly walking in forests magnificent. Landscapes I would never have dreamed of now shelter my voices. I am building them a house of sound. It is magic, magic.

February 19, 1990

On the morning of putting all the pieces together, voices and sound and music, we meet in his office upstairs and Don tells me to "bring the records on the desk." There must be some mistake—Inca flute music and Bach are all I can find. These are for another program, perhaps? No. He has an idea.

I don't believe it. I won't, until he instructs James, the technician, and there begins a dance of James' reaching, pressing, at last, sliding the buttons, recording sound over sound, cued by Don's short finger, a nod, a sudden tightening of his hands. These two have worked together many times and the thing they are creating out of Inca music and Bach and yes, my humble vacuum machine, leaves me shrieking with delight. It is the sound of the boiler, surely this is a wild thing! At the end, when we play it over, it is religious in its majesty.

March 8, 1990

Dear Don:

This is a letter to you tonight, right after I have listened to the broadcast. I feel resonant—a good word for radio, eh? I listened with my best friends—nervous because I didn't know if I would like it after all this time, or how it would sound to them, my kindest critics. And it was a joy and delight from the moment Lister Sinclair said, "Good evening," in that lovely *Ideas* voice.

I couldn't help but smile at the same times when everyone else smiled—and laughed, for they did, sometimes they laughed! And all the rest of the time I smiled too, I couldn't stop smiling, imagining John Donaldson talking about women in the war, shielding his mouth and staying as far away from that damned microphone as possible, or Kathleen Wilkins taking time between a long day of work as an electrician and going home to two kids, telling the jokes the men told on her. I love these people's honesty. I loved listening to them again.

Don, you made a miracle happen tonight—green grass grew on a stone wall—and I thank you with all my heart.

Kate

P.S. When I phoned Heather to ask if the boiler sounded right, she was surprised. "Of course," she said. "Couldn't you hear it breathing?"

This Is What It Seems Like

ZOË LANDALE

This is the moment before

This is the time before beginning
anything
it doesn't matter, doing dishes perhaps,
where day gathers itself into a pounce
    & suspends

I drink tea
Guilty, enjoying it
In the butter-fragrant kitchen,
remains of pancakes clinging to plates
pulpy green innards of blueberries
my daughter has mouthed   & rejected
squashed beads laid along china rims

This is the moment I eye morning
say   *Not yet, I've half a cup left, still steaming*
Northern blue of sky overhead,
tea & deep sky go well together. Autumn
sunshine is passive, thick as apricot preserves

No one will miss this theft

Give us this day our daily tranquility
Afterward comes the Sisyphean struggle
against entropy,
disorder-death of the house,
paint to pick up,
a stop at the credit union
&   *Fresh diaper,* my child requests urgently
Bottle, bottle
The phone rings

This is the time the day's needs
grab   & begin, noisily

Cold tea

KIRSTEN EMMOTT

Labour Pantoum

are we there yet? are we there yet?
this is what it seems like
riding in the back seat of the car
that someone else is driving endlessly

this is what it seems like
sitting long hours by the labour bed
that someone else is driving endlessly
that her labour is bringing to inevitable birth

sitting long hours by the labour bed
with my hand on her brow or her swelling body
that her labour is bringing to inevitable birth
while I, unimportant, look out the window

with my hand on her brow or her swelling belly
the trees and sky slide past
while I, unimportant, look out the window
and I daydream while it all goes by

the trees and sky slide past
as she lies back and rests, eyes closed
and I daydream while it all goes by
then she tenses and pants with a contraction

as she lies back and rests, eyes closed
we are silent in quiet expectation
then she tenses and pants with a contraction
we will be with her for as long as it takes

we are silent in quiet expectation
the night is long, day will soon break
we will be with her for as long as it takes
the city will turn pink with sunrise

the night is long, day will soon break
many babies are born at this hour
the city will turn pink with sunrise
the baby will turn pink with her first breath

many babies are born at this hour
eventually the baby will get to her destination
the baby will turn pink with her first breath
she will travel hopefully, having arrived

eventually the baby will get to her destination
like pulling into your driveway after days on the road
she will travel hopefully, having arrived
this is what it seems like

like pulling into your driveway after days on the road
days spent asking from the back seat
(this is what it seems like—)
"are we there yet? are we there yet?"

GLEN DOWNIE

Hot-house Babies

for Catherine

The hot-house babies sing themselves
lullabies with irregular rhythms.
Not ready yet
is the only lyric they know.

Like kites at the end of their tether, they soon
must fall into the world
or sail away forever out of sight.

We wonder how to hold them
when they are here and not quite here.
So frail and wizened, they've managed a miracle
travelling this far. Unlanded immigrants,
hung up for weeks in customs, they are
suspect refugees, illegal
aliens.

We tell ourselves we will love them
over the threshhold
into existence. Their tiny
troubled footprints
hesitate.

KIRSTEN EMMOTT

Here Be Dragons

she called me sobbing in terror, late at night
help me doctor
there's some awful thing coming out of me
all slimy and smelly
when was your last period, I ask
what? about a week ago
I said, it's a forgotten tampon
go sit on the toilet
use your second and third fingers
reach inside as far as you can
you can always get hold of it
strain down
pull it out
I'll hold the line

long pause
she came back
much calmer now
you were right
this is very embarrassing

don't worry I said
these things happen
you're not the first

well thank you doctor
and we hung up

what times we live in
women come to adulthood,
welcome into their bodies
men, tampons,
birth control devices, IUDs,
and the hands and instruments
of strangers in white coats
—into this important space
not drawn in on the maps;

terra incognita
unknown, unexplored
by the woman who lives there

GLEN DOWNIE

Stroke

Intentions of his limbs, his speech—
all haywire. The sun falters in its arc.
Stages of the cross. The full weight

of what we're doing here
descends. From upstairs,
the watery voices of lovers

quarreling through tears.
I'm no longer young Sunny Jim from the cereal box.
The old man growls at me, alive
in his primitive defences.

GLEN DOWNIE

The Night Man

What do I know about grieving? Not as much
as the night man, who washes again the face
of the hospital moon,

clanging his metal bucket
down the corridors of loss.
Dirty water sloshes over the lip.

It takes a while to die. The soon-to-be widow
switches off thought with TV, lets her heart
glaze over. Not even 30, and already caught
in a Movie-Disease-of-the-Week. Immersed
in the soaps, she learns gestures
she'll need later on.

At the graveside, we are clumsy and green
together; our green hands hold the death
and each other badly. Confused
by this cold passion, I ache to know
what the night man knows,
as she buries
her tear-stained face
in the murky water of my breast.

CHRISTINE MICKLEWRIGHT

Life and Death Around the Vote

The interesting aspect about a labour board vote between two unions, such as the one in my workplace at Canadian Airlines between the CAW and the TCU, is that in the process one has moments of crossing unintentionally into the personal space of co-workers.

My small role in the campaign was the task of contacting all the people in my office who were on a leave of absence, to ensure that they had received a ballot from the labour board and to determine if they had mailed it back. Just the mechanical side, not asking or telling anyone how to vote. Easy stuff I thought.

It was quite different from what I expected.

At first it seemed that I talked to a lot of answering machines, housemates and children. Phones just rang endlessly. Then I began to make connections.

The women on maternity leaves were cheerful, friendly and en- thusiastic. Yes, absolutely, they had their ballots and without my asking, immediately assured me that they had stuffed them back in the mail. Gone, done. Impressive, I thought, with the newborn babes, you'd think that would be the last thing they wanted to contend with. Not so.

I stared long and hard at one name. The image of a weary older woman came to mind. Surely it was more than ten years since she had been in the workplace? Hadn't she retired? I hesitated as I dialled the number, wondering if she was still alive, or if some stranger would answer the phone.

The receiver was picked up slowly. A voice whispered "hello". It was her. She remembered me well. Her voice gathered strength. How delighted she was. Not properly retired yet, she assured me, it would be her 65th birthday next month. Life had taken an upturn lately, now that she has her own motorized scooter to go out into the world on. She was collecting disability benefits, had been for eleven years. And she plunged into the whole saga of how the manager had tried to get rid of her when her health failed. I had forgotten the details, but she brought them back clearly.

More than anything she remembered how the union had supported her and named us all. She then launched into a description of the last union meeting she had attended where a motion was passed that led to the union negotiating a significant improvement to the disability insurance that she, too often, had to rely on.

Lately she has been confused about the bombardment of mail about the union. Well, she's not quite sure. There's the CAW, that's clear. But then there's the TCU. What's that, she wanted to know? I smiled, appreciating her confusion. The union had changed its name from BRAC three years ago. Ah, she said, so who should I vote for? I paused. This is not a campaign call.

I assure her that I cannot tell her who to vote for. She must make that decision herself. She reels off the names of former union executive members and asks which way they are voting and insists on knowing where I stand. I tell her. CAW. She's pleased. I know how to vote now she says.

Then there are the other connections I make. They are sad ones for me. At first I only talk to their answering machines.

Then one by one I hear the weak, slow-paced voices. There are only a few of them. The conversations are brief, they have no energy but I get the information, gently, carefully, and I say goodbye. Inside I wonder if I will ever see them again.

Their voices remind me of the sound of a friend the last time I spoke to him, as he lay dying. We had started work together at the airline on the same day and developed an affectionate friendship. I lost him three years ago.

There is one I cannot reach. For days I can only make contact with a machine. One night, during a quiet moment on my evening shift, I try again, unsuccessfully. I turn to my co-worker and comment on my inability to reach this man. I see his face tighten. And I hear his voice say, "well, he's very, very ill, you know, I don't think he'll ever come back to work."

I feel sick, sick inside as I picture this bright, attractive young man that I have worked with on many occasions. He's one of them too. One of the young men who's dying of this awful disease. Dying because of AIDS.

There are no words to describe this little task that I took on, thinking it would only take moments in my life. But in a week I have felt the miracle of a newborn child, known the satisfied peaceful existence of a retired worker and brushed against the pain and agony in the quiet stillness that hangs just before death claims another young life.

SANDY SHREVE

Telephone Operator

After a few months
the fluorescent glare
fits her with glasses
she'd never needed
before this job

And she begins to see
her supervisors
as grade school
teachers
from whom permission
for basic functions
must be begged:

Even at home
in sleep,
when her bladder
shakes her shoulder
from dreams,
she wakes to her hand
waving anxiously
in the air

PHIL HALL

Mr. White-Out
Carswell Legal
Publishers, Editorial Dept.

—Friday before a long weekend
hour to go till we finish at one
all our copy deadlines met
(slipshod) so I build him

His legs
are the jaws of my staple-remover
his torso
my bottle of *Liquid Paper*

Pulled over the cap:
a rubber thimble
His features on it:
dabs of white-out

His hair can be spiked:
I balance on top of his thimble-head
the husk of a chestnut casing
I've had in my pocket all week (?)

& his arms
can be an unbent paper-clip
taped to the back of the bottle
(like this)

Hey Nance . . .

comes from her cubicle wearing
a card with Ronald Reagan's face on it
her nose through the hole
where his nose should be

Nance/Reagan says s/he likes *Mr. White-Out*
then hands me the card

says *Ron went in for surgery this week
removal of a lesion on his nose*

I put the President's face to mine
put my eye to his nose-hole
as if to a key-hole
as if looking into that brain

& see lawyers talking sports
by the Kodak copying machine

Nearby
one pink *Grow-Wrestler*
floats in a saucer of water
on Katherine's desk

(all week it has bathed
swelling from pill to hero
then been taken out to dry
and shrink from hero
to pill again)

I see the clock (20 minutes left)

I see Ishnan
in her white head-garment
and white chinlette
(most beautiful)

As I pull the President's face off mine
she is saying in her supervisory
conspiratorial whisper *our neighbour
departments are complaining of the noise*

*so let's be professional
kids*

PAM TRANFIELD

Sorry I'm Late

but
I woke up with my period and found
my box of tampons had turned to dandelions,
gone to seed just like on the TV ads.

I left for work, early, in my new ruby slippers
and an awful wind took me from the bus stop
carried me all the way to K-Mart
into the arms of a scientologist
buying oil in the hardware section.
He helped me
find myself, my shoes.

In the elevator
a supervisor smelled my briefcase
told me
tuna sandwiches have been banned
in the secretarial pool.
(I snacked between the 8th and 11th floors
and had to wash my face).

Honestly, I woke up in time but
my Harley-Davidson is missing a cylinder
I had to move Mozart from the shower
I swear the calendar read 1958
the cat knocked over the moon
    I slept in.

KATE BRAID

Recipe for a Sidewalk

Pouring concrete is just like baking a cake.
The main difference is
that first you build the pans. Call them forms.
Think grand.
Mix the batter with a few simple ingredients:
   one shovel of sand
      one shovel of gravel
         a pinch of cement.

Add water until it looks right.
Depends on how you like it.
Can be mixed by hand or with a beater called
a Readi-Mix truck.
Pour into forms and smooth off.
Adjust the heat so it's not too cold,
not too hot. Protect from rain.
Let cook until tomorrow.
Remove the forms and walk on it.

There is one big difference from cakes.
This one will never disappear.
For the rest of your life your kids
will run on the same sidewalk, singing
My mom baked this!

ZOË LANDALE

Only Movement of Your Needle

After twenty years, taste of wintergreen.
  The Irishwoman with calm hands
  who taught Grade Five girls the bright language of thread,
  obsolete, coloured so wonderfully
  you entered eagerly its minute landscape.
Embroidery floss separates three-strand
by three-strand, snarls in your mouth,
six strands   flail   into a lustrous knot.
Blue and delicate, a smocked dress
struggles crisp from its paper pattern.

You want to sew a new heaven.

And the thrift store clothes and the worn clothes
were passed away and there was no more darning.
Everything you are given   needs mending.
Cloth lies limp, in need
of seam to seam transfiguration.
Evenings, only movement of your needle
keeps the world from unravelling.
You take tiny neat stitches: much depends
upon this. Nations.

Creation ever appearing;
your baby strews chaos, you bind it
into neat shelves of teddybears,
stacks of clean laundry.
In the wooden highchair, over porridge,
she smiles wider and wider, includes
you and her, laughing, three new teeth
in a conspiracy   of sudden oatmeal delight.
Weight slips from your stitches;

You taste wintergreen   morning.

KATE BRAID

Concrete Fever

for Phil Vernon

Seven and one half yards of concrete
and every last pebble in place.
A certain kind of concrete steps
I'd never built before, and
six different patio slopes all having to run
with perfect symmetry
to that one post hole marker
of a drain pipe
and an architect antsy eagle eye for the least mistake
or merely visual flaw.

I worried, I cursed, I adjusted and nailed
and bless my soul by six o'clock my steps are a grace to behold
and a joy to ascend
and the water from the hoses
of the concrete finisher
rolls sweetly down all those six slopes
and into that bull's eye drain.
I love water!
I love concrete!
I love the work I did today!

TOM WAYMAN

Did I Miss Anything?

Question frequently asked by students after
missing a class.

Nothing. When we realized you weren't here
we sat with our hands folded on our desks
in silence, for the full two hours

    Everything. I gave an exam worth
    40 per cent of the grade for this term
    and assigned some reading due today
    on which I'm about to hand out a quiz
    worth 50 per cent

Nothing. None of the content of this course
has value or meaning
Take as many days off as you like:
any activities we undertake as a class
I assure you will not matter either to you or me
and are without purpose

    Everything. A few minutes after we began last time
    a shaft of light descended and an angel
    or other heavenly being appeared
    and revealed to us what each woman or man must do
    to attain divine wisdom in this life and
    the hereafter
    This is the last time the class will meet
    before we disperse to bring this good news to all people
        on earth

Nothing. When you are not present
how could something significant occur?

    Everything. Contained in this classroom
    is a microcosm of human existence
    assembled for you to query and examine and ponder

    This is not the only place such an opportunity has been
        gathered

but it was one place

and you weren't here

M.C. WARRIOR

the 1982 roe herring seine fishery (northern area)

attention the roe herring seine fleet!
this is the Fisheries Patrol Vessel Fence Post.
an announcement concerning
a possible opening in Kitkatla
will be made in one half hour.

one hundred thousand horses
steam east.

attention the roe herring seine fleet!
this is the Fisheries Patrol Vessel Com Post.
an announcement concerning
a possible opening in Stryker Bay
will be made in one half hour.

one hundred thousand horses
steam south.

attention the roe herring seine fleet!
this is the Fisheries Patrol Vessel Last Post.
an announcement concerning
an opening in Cumshewa
will be made in five minutes.

one hundred thousand horses
plunge northwest, darkening the sky
and churning Hecate Strait to froth—
two hundred motorized vessels of wrath
seeking to vent on hapless fish
their long month's frustration.

    meanwhile, beneath the quiet waters
      of Cumshewa Inlet,
    the herring school, seeking a private place
    where among the kelps they may embrace.

but on the surface, in the air
sounders and sonars, Cessnas
and helicopters, a whole host
of electronic voyeurs lurks
hoping to cause a massive
coitus interruptus, a wolfpack
waiting for the sentence which spills
a battalion of skiffmen from bunks and galleys,
a barrage of nets from a hundred sterns—
"Cumshewa Inlet is now open."

klaxons shatter eardrums,
searchlights probe each pore
of the shoreline, and deer
flee panic-stricken
from the screams of *"Stand by!"*
a hundred diesels begin to whine
like stukas hungry for cities.

against us, who can prevail?
from so many millions of dollars
worth of steel and technology.
who can hide?

but come daybreak
the shore is white with spawn
while in Vancouver
our creditors are white with shock.

the roe herring seine fleet
    has skunked again.

DAVID R. CONN

On Board Fraser River Tugboats

It's cold and dark at 6 a.m. when RivTow Straits' Fraser fleet makes its daily shift change. A dozen tugs lie at the company's North Arm dock, tied up briefly before dispersing to various jobs along the river.

Among the green-painted vessels is the 35 ft. *Naskeena 4*. Her two crewmen clamber aboard, ready to begin a twelve-hour shift. Rick Jago, the deckhand, lights the galley stove, while skipper Neil Perrault climbs down into the engine room. Twin G.M. diesels clatter into life, but Neil has noticed an exhaust leak below. He decides he can get in some work before the mechanics come on duty at RivTow's repair shop. He calls the company dispatcher on the VHF radio, and we head downriver at full throttle, rolling up a high bow wave at *Naskeena*'s top speed of nine knots.

Neil says people are fascinated by his job. "I give a talk at school every year about what I do, but it's not only the kids. Adults are always saying they'd like to come aboard too." It's not the average deskbound career.

In the tug's boxy wheelhouse, space is at a premium, but visibility is excellent all around. *Naskeena* was designed for river work and built on the river. She's about twenty years old, one of the newer tugs in the fleet.

By 6:30, we're at the Marpole booming grounds, near the Oak Street bridge. Here the river is lined with sawmills and flat booms of logs. *Naskeena* goes to work helping a newer tug, *Westminster Warrior*, to take a boom apart and move some sections across the river. The two skippers meet briefly to study a battered chart board, a sheet of plywood with numbered pieces of tape representing sections of logs.

Rick, wearing rubber caulk boots and a life jacket over work clothes, leaps onto the boom with his pike pole. While he crosses the logs, Neil climbs up to the flying bridge for a better view. Working independently, the two tug crews open the boom and yard out sections to be taken to the opposite bank.

Watching Rick's hand signals, Neil operates the twin throttles and jog steering lever, butts the logs closer to shore so that a tangled boom chain can be released, then turns the tug around and hooks up a length of polypropylene line to tow some sections out. He points to deep dents in the wheelhouse. "Best stay behind the scatter shield. This poly can let go and whiplash."

Neil is forty-five, with fifteen years as a skipper and twenty-five with RivTow. His father was an engineer on the Harrison Lake boats, and he notes there are quite a few second generation towboat hands in the company. Rick is a comparative newcomer, with eleven years working for RivTow or its subsidiaries. Both men prefer the variety of work on the river to "outside." They've been together on *Naskeena* for four years, working one week of day shift, one week off, then one week of nights.

About 8:30, we continue downstream, helping *Warrior* take an eight section boom to a sheeting on Sea Island. Then we turn and run upstream for the home dock. There is plenty of chatter on the two radio sets. One is tuned to the company channel, while the other is used for local communication between tug crews, or switched to an open channel which covers the whole Lower Mainland.

River towing may look placid from shore, but there are many hazards. The close quarters make collision a threat, compounded by traffic, poor visibility, tidal effects or underwater obstacles. In 1975, Neil was skipper on *Naskeena*'s sister ship the night she hit a big deadhead, stopped in the water, and was run down by her own barge. Neil found himself swimming underneath the tow, thinking, "I'm too young to die!"

By 10, *Naskeena* is berthed and being attended by the mechanics. Since repairs may last several hours, Neil elects to take another boat out. The 38 ft. *RivTow Providour* is normally based well upriver at Mission, but has been at the home dock for minor repairs. She was built to move log booms from Howe Sound to Vancouver for Point Grey Towing. Rick knows this boat well, and goes below to start the V-12 G.M. diesel.

In spite of her steerable propellor nozzle, Neil calls the *Providour* "a head boat, not a yarding boat like *Naskeena*." Rick points out that her high bow blocks visual contact while the deckhand is out on the booms and the skipper is in the wheelhouse. Not built for the river, she's been a useful vessel here all the same. As Rick fills up the side tanks with a thousand litres of diesel fuel each, Neil says, "Boats aren't so different, but sometimes you forget which door to use when you need to get up to the flying bridge in a hurry."

By 11:30, we're under way downstream with instructions to assist on a log tow. It takes about half an hour to get down to the North Arm Jetty, near Point Grey. There we meet *Westminster Brave*, struggling with a thirty-six section boom. While Neil maneuvers the *Providour* into position, Rick hooks up the towing wire to a boomstick six sections from the head. With wheel and throttle set, the tug is straining at full speed, but it's like pulling an island. With a combined eight hundred horsepower from the tugs, the tow is making one knot upstream against the ebb tide. It's a good time to eat lunch, since the *Brave* is doing the steering. Over sandwiches, Neil explains that B.C. coast and Fraser tug crews are respected internationally because of the challenging conditions in the region.

At 2:45, the tide has gone slack, and we've towed the boom upstream within sight of the Arthur Laing bridge, near the airport. Then a big Seaspan tug with a loaded barge appears on the starboard bow. Neil and Rick go into action, unhooking the *Providour* from the tow and moving in between barge and boom, ready to shove the barge away if it swings too close.

As soon as the barge is gone, another log boom comes into sight on the port bow, seemingly on a collision course. The *Brave* is already steering the head of our boom to starboard. There is some fast footwork as Neil and Rick hook up at several points in sequence, pulling the whole boom over so that the other one can get by on the inside of the reach. There's no doubt that a quarter-mile long tow could get into a lot of trouble without an assist tug.

As we approach the bridge, *Warrior* arrives to help keep the boom away from the piers, as another tow goes by on the north side of the river. The three tugs negotiate the Oak Street bridge and the swing bridge at Mitchell Island without incident. With the tide now flooding, we're making better time.

At 4:45, Neil leaves the boom and heads for the home dock. We transfer back to *Naskeena* and rejoin the boom with her. Neil says she needs new propeller nozzles, but is basically in good shape. After another hour of towing, we're in Burnaby and approaching our destination, the Byrne Road booming ground. Following radio negotiations with the dispatcher and the crew of the *Brave*, Rick jumps off and splits the boom. At dusk, *Naskeena* shepherds twenty-four sections into position, her masthead spotlights on. The shift completed, we leave *Naskeena* at Comco dock near the booming ground, and her night crew takes over.

M.C. WARRIOR

end of season
"stick, stay, and make her pay"

it is the purpose of night
to disguise, to conceal,
to betray, just

as it is the purpose of foxes
that hens, of soldiers and gangsters
that enemies, and of fall fishermen
that dog salmon should die.

a hunter's moon hangs
like a street lamp
in the clear, cold October sky,
illuminating remote anchorages
in Johnstone Strait where
the year has grown old
and there are neither hens,
nor enemies, nor salmon

only the moon, naked alder
and boatloads of crib-playing
fishermen for whom
the question of betrayal
was settled months ago
and who now ache
only to go home.

Off-Hours

GLEN DOWNIE

the purpose of sleep is industry

the purpose of sleep is not rest
its purpose is industry the furious
construction of a bridge which
fools that we are we destroy
every morning in a flutter of eyelids
in the grope toward a mad buzzing
circle of time the crew are
angel unions from the country of
left-handedness working for love
in their off-hours on the project of
a lifetime with every defeat they resolve
to double production desperate to reach
our side before morning how hauntingly
they plead with us to begin a span of
our own that we all might meet in the center
two arcs one of steel one of matchsticks
an arm's length apart above the river's
torrent the sweat-stained gangs on both sides
eager for a comrade's embrace of victory
while the fearful swaying in the wind and
the white noise of the rapids weakens
our knees prompts our retreat to solid
ground the stone bed where we wake
wondering why we feel so tired
so not-quite-whole

SANDY SHREVE

Laid Off

For years the job has been
within the reach of rolling over
to the early morning news, as close
to her hand as a habit.

One day the second-hand
ticks past six in silence
the old routine, an apparition
hovering in the emptiness

between frantic eyes and yesterday's
fantasy of sleeping in

ZOË LANDALE

I'll go to sea no more

my boat left me
floating high without any ice
forty miles up the Fraser
parting from my order
with the same fine disdain
she would plough through a handful of petrels
in Hecate Strait
petrels who were magically elsewhere
when the thrumming double-ender
reached the spot they'd been
heart-catching birds with hollow bones, forked tails
& soft cries heard in fog

I'll go to sea no more

salt-foolishness this revisionism
of emotion
the curly-haired woman on stage singing
I'll go to sea no more
gym echoing
while I choke up over 7-Up
& cheesies
(every table has two plates of them)

seven seasons I fished
the smell of diesel is like coming home
that boat still churns through my sleep
white & red, varnish gleaming
sometimes I'm headed for the rocks,
others I'm terrified I'll tangle the lines
tangle them definitively
unbelievably, it will be a disaster of colossal
proportions, my loss will be blazoned
across an orange horizon for the whole fleet
to gossip over
trolling bells dinging wildly
flashers, spoons in a silver, brass

pink & green knot
gurdies straining at their bolts,
stainless wire spun off the gurdies
& ripped all the way down
to backing
heartlines of husband, home, work
zing, gone, all of them,
leaving cut-outs in air
my eyes strain, a moment ago there was a red shirt
a man with a curly beard wearing it, truly

& for that abandonment there is no untangling
only forgiveness
    Hey, you caught North America
hooks into submerged mountain tops
you & your boat towing the world
at 700 rpm
momentarily

in the gym
no one is dancing yet
the woman on stage sings   *I'll go to sea no more*
the lights are dim, blue
& the man who fathered my child
sits across the table from me,
his hand there
for the taking, warm as a shoe
you put off for a moment by the door
intending to go outside again;
the leather remembers heat
there is that moment of unexpected comfort
when you put it back on

in our house across the road from the Fraser,
the fleet moves masts, wishbone poles
by our front window
temporarily framed, the tingling geometry
of winches & stays
I'll go to sea no more   but it is
all right
I carry salt chuck back of my eyes
& I have put on   solid ground

KATE BRAID

Pass the Pain

for Eleanor Knight

My muscles grow taut from physical work
and what do they learn
from all this clenching?
To send my hands numb every morning,
a twist of pain in my back,
the strain
of an eternally aching shoulder.

I lay this imbalanced body, an offering
on the masseuse's table.
Her hands and shoulders, strong
like mine, work
to lift the knots of muscles brittle with armour.

But where does the hurt go as it seeps
from my skin into hers?
What pains of mine does she carry home
at night?
Who takes her tired shoulders
after a day of blessing the rest of us,
and gives her ease?
Where does this long cycle of aching
end?

GLEN DOWNIE

The Steps

At the end of a working day,
self-doubt: existential
five o'clock shadow.

Slogging up the twilight streets, you find
scorched lawns, trees
smoking like oil lamps. The raven
wing of your heart
beats fitfully.

And a black stone by your gate becomes
the cat, all tucked under itself
like a dark-baked loaf. Hearing you,
the stone opens its yellow eyes. Never
has the sky borrowed just that colour before,

the amber of insect prisons, or white-hot
metals cooling. The house feels clenched
in its darkness. Perhaps
someone no longer loves you. One
by one by one, you take the steps.

PAM TRANFIELD

Holiday. 1988.

1. Montana

as if the mountains aren't enough
to remind us
of our fragility;
white crosses on the highways
markers for every person
killed in every accident

2. Idaho

a shirtless man wearing sandals
pulls a crucifix
along the shoulder of the highway;
the woman in the car ahead
eating a corn dog waves at him
honks her horn
drops the corn dog
bows her head to find it
crosses into the opposite lane;
her bumper sticker says
Jesus is Watching

she hits a fence
jumps out of the car laughing
thanking the Lord
for life;
the man with the cross
walks on.

DAVID R. CONN

Homage: St. Francis Fair

It was at the country fair
they performed the old feat.
The wire had been duly strung
well above the muddy grounds.

The family took turns
stepping across, in white
against the overcast.
Hardly anyone noticed, below.

There was a white cross
high on the scarp behind.
A boy had fallen, long before.
They were taking that chance.

I heard a motorcycle overhead.
Yes, the family balanced there,
the finale that commanded attention,
stately progress along the wire.

I forgot the troupe until
I had to cross a crane boom
on a catwalk without railings.

Careful steps. Perfect posture.
(The cool breeze above the harbour)
Concentration like an aura,
watching well ahead, not below.

I learned how intensely
the family had lived on the wire,
only balance to save them,
all for our entertainment.

M.C. WARRIOR

on position—Kyoquot

dreams of pine and granite
fin silverbright
in the Kyoquot rain,
splash lazily
across a closed inlet.

marsh grass sways
in a slow current, geese
and crabs nibble
on our breakfast scraps,
and the dog salmon leap
into our glacial dream.

in a closed area
i bleed:
in a closed inlet
i watch pine growing
down through granite:
in a closed area i dream
of geese and deer and barbara
while a grey sky leaches
the colour from my arms:
in a closed inlet
i watch my fingers erupt,
itch, dream
of pine and granite
flashing lazily
in the Kyoquot rain.

they dream of an opening
which will fin silverbright
through the inlet and close
my season for the balance.

SANDY SHREVE

Surfaces

The hollow scrape of blades
moves skaters through crisp air
this cold, a particular winter
where toques and scarves and gloves
are superfluous as buttons,
jackets flap in the wind
of our movements

so many trajectories
a community singing on ice
the lake almost large enough, people make space—
pucks and sticks
pause for these wobbly legs to pass
and no one points to laugh;
the only borders here
are where lifeguards have hacked at the ice,
checked for thickness and roped off
spots too thin for safety

we slide or glide or stumble
away from treacherous areas
into indiscriminate welcomes
to all who venture onto the lake:
this surface beneath our feet
the only skin of concern

In the centre of a city
echoes of unhurried sound
take me back to the Tantramar
redwings in the rushes
their harmonica call a microcosm
of what I miss

what is it about place that seeps
into your soul
mindless of miles, however far you move—
plays out the string and holds you
tempts a false nostalgia:

I catch myself believing
this momentary release from rancour
holds the possibility of a city
reclining into country life, as if back home
there was never anything like a frozen pond
abandoned to power, boys
claiming ownership of the top, slap shots
tripping girls' attempts at circles. . .

At some point every conversation
comments on the relief
of outdoor skating: no one dictating
now to the right, the left,
backward only, just couples,
muzak piping out the pace

our music is disparate voices
mingled with the language of blackbirds
ducks and crows, our patterns as random
and predictable as their flight:
wings slant and turn snug in the sky
feet sculpt curves and crossroads into ice

Such a freeze is rare here. The need
to get to the middle, irresistible
just to see what it's like to look
at the path from the lake for a change

searching for perspective, almost everyone
explores the iced-in cattails and reeds
where the heron hunts when it's water
where we turn from relics of summer
locked in the frozen surface:
styrofoam, cellophane, plastic trash
lost tennis balls and toys

all over the place

we look without seeing
how fragile our smiles
when it's youths who feel free
to nod to the aged, whites to
the black or the brown
then skate or stroll away
from subtle assumptions behind
who welcomes who

we sing in the same
clutches and gaggles as ever
leaving implications, like our litter
for someone else to face

SANDY SHREVE

A Pair of White Ducks

A noose of opaque plastic
Two birds, one trapped in hours
of panic: Feathered waves.

Someone's hand tossed that collar
into calm water, cracked
open the can and raised it
to a peaceful evening

a small act
in the scheme of things

like children playing by the lake
daring the speed of their hands
against sprigs of parched grass
lit with matches

it's the flame that gets away
ignites a whole field
It could as easily have been anyone's
and you're indignant
when blamed

just as it isn't you
who's polluted this lagoon
where fishers toss their lines
for trout, imagine
edible fish.

Casting, incessant
as the hoarse mourning
of a lone white duck

TOM WAYMAN

The Politics of the House: Chairs

Any chair is a success
if it can support a woman or man

without collapsing.
Chairs may be padded, or bare, shaped wood,

foldable, stackable
or reclining. Yet each

in its prime is our ally:
who isn't grateful for

an opportunity to sit down?
Of course there are renegade chairs—

hard and uncomfortable
making a meeting, lecture

or even a dinner party
unendurable.

Also, there are office chairs
designed to be below the height

of one other person's chair in a room
to intimidate us,

to teach us what the owner of these chairs
thinks is our place.

Yet outlaw chairs
are the exception,

are in no way representative
of chairdom. Chairs are the essence

of what befriends us on this planet.
We travel greater distances in chairs,

for instance, than on beds
or even our own feet.

And although many of the tasks
we have to do to keep the world going

are performed standing up,
an enormous number get accomplished

while we are seated.
And other jobs could be:

after years of doctors trying to force us
to give birth on our backs, for example,

we have begun to return
to a more natural position—

using a birthing stool, the chair
of life. In fact, chairs adopt the attitude

of the Earth toward humanity:
ever-present, neutral toward our individual achievements

but generally hospitable
to the endeavors of our species.

For these reasons
it is easy to comprehend why

some primitive tribes buried their dead
in a sitting position.

After all, if there is a life beyond this one,
probably in that existence, too,

more will have to be done seated
than stretched out—loafing or sleeping.

What does seem mysterious
is why none of these early peoples

developed a burial chair.
Such an object obviously would represent

a veneration owed the most useful human construct.
No doubt such artifacts are absent

because unlike weapons, pottery, jewelry
or anything else found in ancient graves

chairs are too valuable
to mail on to the next world.

DAVID R. CONN

Scenes at the Wake

for Bob Holroyd

In his kitchen
the mood is relaxed, as if
the host has stepped out
for a cigarette.

In his bedroom,
there are no illusions.
I have worn the clothes
of the dead proudly,
but the stacks of shirts
offered up are final evidence.

In his living room,
a candlelight filigree
of photographs and flowers:
a humanist shrine.

Throughout his house,
music. A man transformed
lumber toward song
in his tiny shop.

Now he is gone
music remains—
the sweet tone
of handmade guitars.

Room for All

KATE BRAID

'Girl' on the Crew

The boys flap heavy leather aprons at me
like housewives scaring crows
from the clean back wash.
   Some aprons. Some wash.
They think if the leather is tough enough
if the hammer handle piercing it is long enough
I will be overcome with primordial dread
or longing.

They chant construction curses at me:
   Lay 'er down! Erect those studs!
and are alarmed when I learn the words.
They build finely tuned traps, give orders I cannot fill
then puzzle when a few of their own
give me pass words.

I learn the signs of entry,
dropping my hammer into its familiar mouth
as my apron whispers *O-o-o-h Welcome!*

I point my finger and corner posts spring into place
shivering themselves into fertile earth at my command.
The surveyors have never seen such accuracy.

I bite off nails with my teeth
shorten boards with a wave of my hand
pierce them through the dark brown love knots.
They gasp.

I squat and the flood of my urine digs
whole drainage systems in an instant.
The boys park their backhoes, call their friends
to come see for themselves or they'd never believe it.

The hairs of my head turn to steel and join boards
tongue-in-groove
like lovers along dark lanes.

Drywall is rustling under cover
eager to slip over the studs at my desire.

When I tire, my breasts grow two cherry trees
that depart my chest
and offer me shade, cool juices
while the others suck bitter beans.

At the end of the day the boys are exhausted
from watching.
They fall at my feet and beg for a body like mine.
I am too busy dancing to notice.

CHRISTINE MICKLEWRIGHT

Room for All

Shift work. It can be a gross interference with your life or it may allow you to do things you wouldn't do otherwise. For those who must plan their lives around it, especially the rotating shifts, working can be a daily scramble to find order.

This is the week I struggle in early. Up at 3:30 a.m. A cool dark and lonesome hour. Out on the road by 4:30 a.m., speeding on empty roads, cursing red lights and praying for green.

Sliding my car into the parking lot. Zipping my security card into some electronic slot that winks green and releases the door for my entry. Barely on time, but there's no one to notice.

The long room is crowded with green glowing VDTs. The chairs are, for now, empty. Soon voices will clatter, chatter and clash around the machines that now sit silently, or emitting the occasional beep.

Touching keys and entering the system, it greets me, demanding I read this or that. I plunge on, printing flight schedules, checking arrivals and departures. Talking to voice recording machines telling the callers of planes coming and going. Sometimes I hear them roar overhead, see their wheels poised for touchdown, gliding in, climbing out.

Then suddenly I am no longer alone. Other shapes slip in, sign in, talking, laughing, or drifting in glazed silence. My co-worker begins his day with a gentle sigh. A relief agent, his schedule is always haphazard. Today he is happy, he has a day shift, but the rest of the week is all wrong, all evenings. This must not be and he begins the begging, pleading, bartering process with fellow workers in the great shift exchange game.

"I guess you want to be home with your family in the evening?" I inquire gently.

"Yes," he responds with a happy smile. "But more than that, I must go to the Mosque each evening."

"The Mosque—every day?" my lapsed Catholic existence injects a tone of astonishment into my voice. Once a week on Sundays was bad enough for me.

"Yes," he informs me, solemnly. "It gives me peace. It's only a short visit for maybe an hour, but it soothes my soul and gives me the inner tranquility that I need."

Images and memories tumble through my mind. Purple dawns ruptured by wailing calls for prayer broadcast by tinny speakers that have long since replaced men in minarets. Silent black shapes swirl along dusty sidewalks, the women in purdah, eyes watching from behind a crocheted lace grill, hidden from the lustful glances of men. The discomfort of a western woman standing revealed, prey to passing hands.

And I have to ask him: what of Salman Rushdie, his death sentence?

He smiles and shakes his head. "I follow Aga Khan. Our beliefs are more moderate, more modern, especially," he grins at me, "where women are concerned. As for Khomeini and Rushdie, no, this matter I do not agree with. It solves nothing."

The supervisor hovers around. Some problem is discussed and resolved, then a pause as a fellow worker interrupts with a phone message for me from some civil servant in immigration. And my supervisor is suddenly ablaze with a barely suppressed rage.

"Immigrants! It's time it was all stopped. They're abusing the system, arriving here without documents pretending to be refugees. The scams they get away with. Look at those Sikhs coming in on that boat in Nova Scotia, lying about where they came from, just to get in. All those Asians coming in every day and legitimate people wait years or can't get in at all."

I am at first stunned at this newly-exposed aspect of this little fellow. Then I am angry and there is an uncomfortable debate. "It's not like that at all," I say, trying to explain the myths and confusion about refugees and immigrants and the contributions they make to our country. My words are wasted.

My friend sits silently, staring at his computer. I realize I know little about him other than I think he could be from India, because of his accent, yet I am not sure. I know he visits relatives in Bombay, so I begin to explore his world and I am surprised.

I learn about the boyhood of this man, growing up in Nairobi. His father died when he was three and his mother raised the family alone. He mourns for the childhood he never had. Each morning up at 4 am and out on the streets selling samosas (pyramid shaped deep fried curried potatoes) before school and then again at the end of the day. All to make a little bit of money to help the family. His family origins are somewhat murky, perhaps Iran, perhaps India and it was several generations earlier.

"Some days," he recalls, "there was no food at all." Clothing was scarce and living was hard. He compares it now to the life of his children, a fourteen-year-old daughter and an eight-year-old son, all comfortable in this Canadian lifestyle. It is his wife who is from Bombay, the relatives are in-laws. India is not his country although the life of the poor there parallels his own upbringing on another continent.

I feel it and taste it. How many early mornings did I tramp the crowded streets of India, through five adventurous months nearly twenty years ago? Sidewalks of blanketed bodies, huddled for warmth, all their possessions clutched tightly beside them. In my hungry search for breakfast, there would always be some grubby street corner where a young boy plied his wares. "Samosas Memsahib", he would cry out, thrusting them into my hands. And I would ache for him, for this child that could not play, that must work for his family to live.

And I stare at the back of my retreating supervisor and feel the anger. The rage against those who have it all and would keep it from those in need. These people live on phoney fears, terror of takeover, of some unnamed loss, those selfish white supremists that would keep this country sparse for themselves.

On the long plane trips to Ottawa each month, trekking my way east for a meeting about employment and immigration, I am always struck by the vastness of the land, uninhabited, sparsely populated areas contrasted with crushing, crowded, lively cities. I know there's room for all and room for more.

My co-worker turns from a conversation with another worker. He's grinning again. "This is a good week," he declares, "God is looking after me, all my night shifts are gone. Now I have day shifts. I can go to the Mosque every night. My family will be so happy."

I share his elation, even if I cannot begin to imagine such religious commitment. Just for a moment I flash back to a seat on a grubby steam train hissing in an Indian railway station. "Trains may either make up or lose time" says the sign. I am tempted to put that on the flight information recorder, sure would save a lot of bother whenever Time Air (which we pretend is Canadi>n Airlines) has a problem with one plane and messes up the schedule for the rest of the day.

In my mind I see myself hanging out the window of the soot-covered train reaching towards the hands of a young Indian boy on the platform. Coins drop into his palm and I take two hot samosas from his small brown fingers. His gleaming white teeth beam up at me, then he turns quickly to his next customer.

I smile at my co-worker, relieved that he has left that terrible poverty behind. But I cannot calm my anger towards those who will not willingly share the wealth and opportunity of this nation.

For there is room for all of us.

PAM TRANFIELD

On the Job for Jesus

I had Jesus on the line today
He lost his SIN card
somewhere overseas.

Times have changed for Jesus,
a tabernacle on Hastings Street
wants to make a video of his life
He will not work for free.

Jesus said
I can't get paid without my number,
man does not live by bread alone.

I told him to find his work permit
and fill out a form at the office downtown.

He thanked me
asked me my name   said
come see me sometime
I got 120 channels on my converter
most of them are blank
don't get hardly nothing.

KATE BRAID

Think Like a Weightlifter, Think Like a Woman

First day on the job and the foreman orders
in a voice like a chainsaw,
Hoist those timbers
by hand to the second floor.
Crane's broken down.

I keep my mouth shut
with difficulty, knowing
how much a six-by-six timber
twelve feet long and fresh
from the Fraser River, knowing
how much it weighs.

Lorne, my partner, says nothing,
addresses the modest mountain of timbers
towering over our heads, smelling
sweetly nostalgic for forest.

Weighing in with the wood he faces,
with a belly like a great swelling bole,
he shakes off my motion to help and
bends as if to pick up a penny,
scoops up the timber and packs it, 50 feet,
to lean against the damp grey sides
of the concrete core.
When he doesn't look back,
it's my turn.

And now, because I need this job, and
because it's the first day and because
every eye is watching The Girl,
I bend my knees as the book says,
think like a weightlifter, take the beam
by its middle and order my body
to lift.

Reluctantly, the great tree, sweating pitch,
parts with its peers with a sucking sound,
and the beam and I sway to the designated spot,
I drop it. Repeat.

Alone, I carry beams to Lorne
who alone heaves them with the slightest grunt
to the labourer who bends from the second floor
with a hurry-up call,
Faster! Faster!

No. I will never be a carpenter, I think, *never
able to work like these men.* Then
Lorne falters.
Without thinking I reach up my two arms beside him
and push with all my might.
The beam flies to the second floor and mindless,
I turn to fetch him another.

Without a word
Lorne follows me back to the pile,
lifts one end and helps me
carry the next timber to the wall.
Without a word we both push it up,
continue this path together
find a rhythm, a pace
that feels more like dancing.

Lorne says, *You walk different. Yes.*
For on this day I am suddenly
much, much stronger, a woman with the strength
of two.

SANDY SHREVE

Companion

This machine is advertised
as a companion: personal
computer
or perhaps I misunderstand
and the innuendo implies
status.

Neither interpretation is real:
it takes up space in my office
but it is in fact, mere
mechanical apparatus,
a replacement part in the false
hierarchy of jobs

an absence
of someone else's hands
sharing the full range of work
side-by-side with mine

CHRISTINE MICKLEWRIGHT

Getting It Down Pat

Mind numbing PAT Library
   the words on the VDT
   blur and scramble;
   my head aches
   my mind jumbles
   the words that glare
   green on the screen.

Pegasus Assisted Training
   computer-teach
   spewing airline lingo,
   friendly PAT
   go slow or fast
   learn at any speed,
   it promises,
   he promises

Who is he?
   this PAT who claims to be male,
   who dares to affront me
   with sexist travel questions
   I refuse to answer:
   "Where would you go to get 'leid'?"
   My error factor rises.

State of the art ed.
   tech change, self instruction
   no longer the screech of chalk
   or rustle of flip charts
   just deathly silence
   broken only by fingers tapping keys
   with only the barest hint of an instructor

It doesn't seem to matter if
   I'm right or wrong
   the keys I hit, the responses;
   just get through the lesson

and on to the next,
PAT urges me to type
"skip to" and the lesson number.

And my classroom companion
skips faster than I,
too fast surely,
am I so slow, so stupid?
and he laughs at me
slamming the enter key
over and over
and his lesson still
chugs by
with or without his answers;
no one knows, no one cares.

Except me, struggling through,
diligently doing it all,
hating PAT, his arrogance
his "male world"
I want a real person
with a blackboard
for encouragement,
for feedback
for a sense of completion.

But there's only PAT
teasing us all in the classroom;
I can take no more
of this non-learning
so I skip to my lou
and I'm out.
It's over.
PAT myself on the back.

PHIL HALL

(guide to executive suicide)

Shoot yourself
in the foot

Put your foot
in your mouth

Put your money
where your mouth is

Shoot your mouth off

M.C. WARRIOR

grievance meeting

for the manager it's much like chess
—a canny player profits
even from a loss. he bears
no grudges, only the urge
to play again soon
with different pieces.

for the organizer it's like a stroke
—the final burst of clarity
crippling an already
numbed skull. victory
is always fleeting: defeat,
like income tax, inevitable.

for the crewman, it's going home
to explain there are other boats,
other companies, and other jobs
          in other cities.

M.C. WARRIOR

see you on the grounds

Jack and i were salmon
and herring buddies until
the boat was sold,

the kind you become
on the grounds when you fish
together year after year:
the kind who hit the bars
in Rupert, Hardy Bay, and Tahsis
to bullshit about the kids, music,
the union, and the state of the world,
but who somehow never get around
to seeing each other in town,
except perhaps for a beer
after a Local meeting.

in Seal Cove i heard
that he'd slipped
on some hydraulic oil
while bringing the rings
around the stern,
fell hard, bouncing
off the rail to the deck,
never letting them go.

he's not worked since,
living on a small pension
from Compo and what his wife
makes at the cannery.
occasionally he comes down
to the netloft for what he calls
his exercise. the last time
i saw him, we were loading
the inside seine. we bullshitted

with him a bit and i asked
how he was making out. as he left
i called after him, without thinking,
"see you on the grounds."

PAM TRANFIELD

Mrs. Terreli

200 dollars a week I get from Canada Packers and now I get this letter from you people you tell me I can't get UIC because I got this pension. Yes company pension. I'm not 65 yet but I'd be better off. I pay into pension and I pay into UIC since 1946 when I start. Never worked nowhere else. Started off on the line packaging bacon then they move me up to the front to cashier in the plant. Now I'm out of a job. Line work was the best but my back bothers me see. Oh all that leaning down and stretching out your arms. Yes I worked all day but we were young. You don't mind that so much when you're young. It was a place I liked to work. One girl I started with we got laid off together that was four weeks ago and I don't get no money since. She's 65 but I'm only 63. Oh I've looked, I've looked a dozen places every day but who hires a cashier when the young girls look pretty and take half the pay what I ask for. I still want to work. I have to work. Yes I was working union. Walked into Woodward's but they pension their cashiers off at 61. Started off paying 25 cents a week into UIC when I left it was $13 a week off my paycheque. And you people say I can't collect any of it. I guess there's nothing I can do. I just wanted to tell you I think I'm entitled to something after all this time.

KIRSTEN EMMOTT

Isaac

Isaac's not stopped yelling
since I delivered him.
Placed in his mother's arms, he yelled,
she smiled weakly, turned her head away.
"I'm so tired," she whimpered. In labour
she was like a heavy sack, obstinate and immobile.

Wendy bustles round her, tidies the sheets,
puts Isaac in the crib. I go over to him.

Did I hurt him with the forceps?
My back's to the room as I lean over Isaac.
His eyes are tight shut against the light.
I slip my finger into his mouth
and he quiets at once, sucks strongly,
peeks out of one eye; I shade his face;
he opens the other eye, dark like his mother's.

We study one another. I grin widely.
He sucks my finger and we say hello,
nobody watching us, we're alone together.

I feel like I've sneaked off from
some noisy, jampacked party
to the kitchen, where behind the door
I'm kissing someone else's husband.

KIRSTEN EMMOTT

Theota's Labour

I've brought the gown I'm sewing.
The yellow satin passes through my hands;
stitch, stitch, and I sew the pieces together.
I must pass the time,
I must sit silent on the floor
while Theota labours,
supported by her friends,
walking up and down
or lying or squatting;
loving hands rub her back
but we all labour fruitlessly,
for the child won't come.
I can see that;
I can see the waiting hospital,
the anesthetic, the scalpel,
the child born into *my* hands,
but I can't speak,
I can't step into the flow
I can't put my hands on Theota's body
until she invites me.

Soon, now, she'll turn to me.
Stitch, stitch, and I sew my waiting shut.

GLEN DOWNIE

Survivors: The Mother

Well and whole, she was a part
of his slow blue dying.
She prayed and wept, her heart
following him to the end
of the earth for a cure. Why
should miracles always be distant,
something so different from where
and who we are? She remembers
him coming back, after
the miracle had failed,
wearing a nautical flag on his chest
that warned: *Stay away! I'm on fire
and have dangerous cargo on board.*
She flung her arms around that fire,
crushed it to her,
and she is burning still,
though he is gone.

GLEN DOWNIE

Survivors: The Sister

In the bald fact of his death at 20,
she confronts the underside
of the grand design: a mare's nest
of fine black threads; a circuit apparently
hard-wired for static. The whispers

of well-intentioned friends offer her
all the reassurance of a dry broom
sweeping it under the rug. *And yet*, she thinks

perhaps they're right—that by and by
a meaning may emerge. I've known scars
to assume the shapes of letters,
seen cracks in the wall
slowly become a face.

But for now, there is only bafflement
and an undiminishing ache
as night after night
the angel of irrational numbers
visits. Picking the lock
of her heart, he steals
into her dreams. Through the hollow hours
she weeps beneath the shelter
of his broken wings.

PAM TRANFIELD

Flight

She calls for me from a nest of pillows
using the name of a long dead sister
whose picture hangs beside the bed.

She asks for her calendar, draws a line through yesterday,
and turns pages to the month that has a picture of an eagle.
She tells me she will be 98 in that month,
asks if I remember the eagles that took hens on father's farm;
I say that I do, and that breakfast is almost ready; she smiles
anticipating eggs.

GLEN DOWNIE

Ron and Don

Called to your dying twin, you will not
stay. Duty, pity, can compel
only so much. I do
a double-take coming out of his room
seeing him in you, fleshed out
like a second chance.

You go in, talk perhaps ten minutes,
then you're back, saying
he wants sleep and you want
lunch. You're satisfied
with one glance in the distorted mirror.
It's enough—one terrible glimpse
of how you may end.

But an instant later, he's yelling
Where's my brother? protesting
he only closed his eyes for a moment.
You turn, mouth twitching the twitch *his* mouth makes
under stress. The look you wear
says *What does he want from me?*

Later, you wonder aloud who'll tie up his affairs,
wanting someone, anyone but yourself
to get things done. *I don't know his life*
out here, don't know his friends.
We haven't been close. . . . And can't bear to be
close now. Close as two halves of
a cancer cell dividing. Close as
the rhymed syllables of your names.

KIRSTEN EMMOTT

Mrs. Copp

Marion Copp
whose courage and cheerfulness
is a lesson to us all
who will die because I found her cancer too late,
who will be my first patient to die,
everyone else being too young or too lucky or too tough,
whose approaching death is rushing at me
like the next dip in the rollercoaster,
whom I visit every week
not only for her
but for penance because I found her cancer too late,
has a little room in the nursing home
hung with knitted ornaments and toys,
signs in big letters, all she can see now,
phone numbers, addresses, including mine,
but to me they read:
"Nice view of the park, isn't it?
Memorize it. And us, too,
the bag of yarn, the talking clock.
We'll be around.
You won't forget us."

GLEN DOWNIE

The Book of the Dead

Housekeeping proves that death is always with us. Every month at the clinic, a list comes round and I'm expected to prune from my files the names that are mine: Leo, Shirley, Alfred, Enid, Stan. . . . Most of us say we hate this part of the job, when we're temporarily reclassified: ASSISTANT GRIM REAPER. I try to see it instead as a spiritual discipline, a chance to develop my latent angelic nature.

I confess I haven't the heart to use the trashcan. Month after month, I ferry those souls to a big, black binder I call The Book of the Dead. There they can reminisce alongside their neighbours in the new development. It helps them—and me—not to feel so suddenly lost.

If I'm in this work much longer, I'll need Volume II. One day we will all be forgotten; I know I'm just stalling for time. But when I go, I plan to take The Book with me, to bring to God's notice the lives of his suffering people. Fiercely exasperating people, some of them, who I think of now with great fondness. *These are my dead*, I say to myself, conscious of a strange possessiveness. Ironic, since the truth of it is that I am the one possessed—by their irascible voices reciting to me the litany of their troubles, garrulous to the end, and loath to leave.

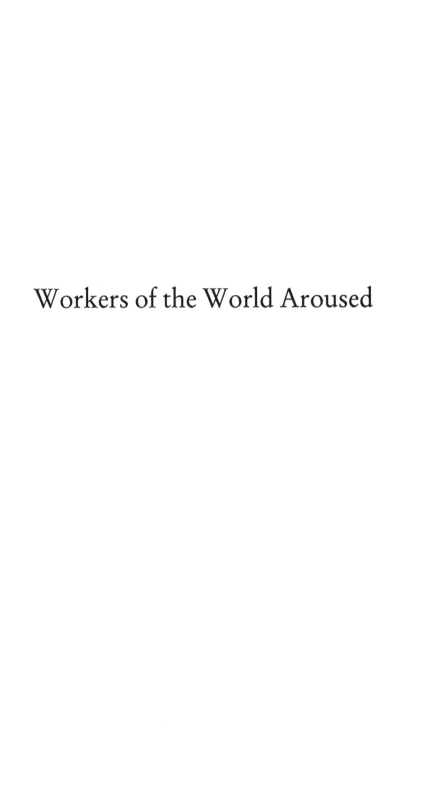

Workers of the World Aroused

KATE BRAID

Class Conscious

I put my hands on the table
right after you noticed the hammers
I wear for earrings.
An accidental gesture
     sort of.
The hands that yield a hammer
I wanted to show you
so there'd be no illusions
about me
     tough woman
     tough hands.
I didn't want you to get the wrong idea
about me
     looking so feminine in some parts.
What you see
my hands say for me
is what you get.

I put my hands on the table
tentative
proud   sort of
hoping you are one of the ones
who likes a working hand

and scared you're not.

KIRSTEN EMMOTT

Short Man

fortunately I was masked
nothing showing but my eyes
still you can tell a lot from eyes
o.r. nurses know this,
concentrate all their beauty
in their expert lashes,
their pearlized shadow.
sloe-eyed under bouffant paper caps
they peek out of
green cotton purdah
promising a harem of delights
to male surgeons.
we, the women doctors
are ignored eunuchs
slowly waving our fans
over the surgeon's beaded brow. . .

well, I was early,
as a junior doctor ought to be,
ready gowned and gloved
when he entered, holding his hands up
fresh from the scrub sink;
I handed him the towel
then held out the gown
and he thrust in his arms

he was much shorter than I
my arms went round his neck
I wrapped him in his green sterile gown
his arms went round me
like a bridegroom
he did not allow
his sterile sleeves to brush my sides
he did not allow
his ungloved hands to touch me
we stood embracing in germfree purity

he looked up at me
brown eyes over the paper mask
I wonder if he saw
my pupils dilate

hastily I dropped the gown
on his shoulders
the scrub nurse came
to snap up the back

I moved to my side of the patient
my hands shook
as I picked up the instruments

PAM TRANFIELD

Bill's Underwear

one wanted to write like Hemingway
the other was proud of his past
in a motorcycle gang
a third lived in garages
i worshipped him from afar
we almost made love once
but he stopped
to comfort his dog

such language i learned from these men
Satan's Choice liquor delivery
head-space

none of these men
wore underwear
they all wanted to be
on top
as i lay passive
tangled in their past
and present

i thought of them all
this morning
when i saw you
in your underwear
yawning over a sink of dishes
waving me back to bed
to wait for breakfast.

ZOË LANDALE

Song of the Second Mouth

I am a door. In my recesses are the mysteries. Enter at the danger of losing your way along the way: I am vastly larger than you believe, and more ancient. In me is fragrant smoke, licking orange of flames, glow of the hearth. Come to me hungry and I will feed you, thirsty and I will give you drink. I am wild grape. Suck me and pulp will pucker cool against your tongue.

Doors are meant to be opened. Come. I am slick velvet and cave, far and dark beneath the mountain. Don't be afraid of the bones, they're old. They blaze splendidly, femurs erect as the pale phalli of moths. Deeper, come down deeper.

Opened is honest. That much you can expect from me, no more. I will lie to you with rooms and phantoms but with my pink and varied tongues you can expect a mouth ready to meet yours. I will give you all sorts of roses, damask, tea, cabbage and moss, but only one name: guard it and your face will probably stay the same. I cannot say for sure. Honest is the pink of cloud ribbon as the sun goes down behind jagged triangles of scrub evergreen. I am the going down of the sun, your dark wanting. I know you by the intensity of your need; I flush from your blind bright desire and hate myself for it. I am response.

I am the swelling of the evergreen cones, the slippery yieldedness of rosy galloping around firelight. Sheen of me opened, that raised sweet ecstasy of asking, What is it you *really* want? to please in high breaking waves that tumble over and over to quiescence and building again.

Firelight is how you will remember me, assured as warmth from glowing fir logs, as ephemeral. You think you make me, stick upon branch, that burning depends on the fuel you bring in your arms, but I will flame or darken according to what holiness possesses my will. You come to worship: it is well.

In firelight, the evergreens are black, robbed of colour. I have opened to you in the guise of being honest, said Come, try the door. You can leave when you will.

DAVID R. CONN

Adagio

The long sigh of rain
fades and crescendos
on the window,
heard and unheard as
our hands twitch, grasping
the edges of dreams.

When we stormed
our side of the glass,
night clamoured.
Now it plays
the dark mirror, void
full of silver droplets.

In pale distances
of sleep, I fall,
twisted and burning.
Too many secrets.
You and the rain quench me
like murmurous clouds.

M.C. WARRIOR

night watch

white foam
on a black swell,
a new moon
and Jordan River astern,
nothing but ghosts
on the radar.

> carefully,
> cat-like I bite
> the nape of your neck,
> the arch of your throat,

then stroll onto the dodger
to check the running lights,
and time Sheringham
as it winks lasciviously
at the american shore.

GLEN DOWNIE

Nova

After loving,
wisps of damp hair cling
like steamed chrysanthemum petals
to your brow.

The refrigerator hums
and I hear the ringing of stars
out beyond Andromeda.

For every orbit winding down
somewhere a new sun blushes into sight.
Soundlessly, our rumpled bed
drifts toward its rightful place in the cosmos.

Curved to each other in sleep,
we are two spoons nestled in a drawer.

TOM WAYMAN

Modifications to the Heart

In a child, the heart is plump
but strong with the tenseness
of young limbs.
Occasionally, though, an event
will tear open the covering of the organ
like a knee scraped bloody in a spill from a bicycle.
The wound is painful for days,
then heals completely.

Yet insecurities
or a hideous incident or situation
involving the boy or girl
can grip the heart
and twist it
to a barely recognizable shape.
Thus the modification of the heart
may commence early—the organ might or might not
ever recover its whole function.

And for each person there awaits a first
betrayal or loss
usually experienced in adolescence
that permanently marks the heart,
even if the only evidence years later
is a slight nick or scar.
Thereafter, the blows begin to strike
with increasing rapidity
in the normal course of adult love
and rejection.
Mostly these assaults
result in bruises and other surface discolouration
that disappear in time
but underlying tissue also can be injured.
The latter damage, as with some childhood hurt
that weakened subsurface muscle and fibres,
might be undetected for years

until a portion of the heart one Thursday after a meal
collapses.

And from time to time, a wound is inflicted so deeply
—either in a single moment
with a sharp blow like a knife's
or in a jagged tear
ripped slowly apart during weeks or months
of excruciating pain—
that medical intervention is required.
This can take the form of stitches
or a metal or plastic plate must be implanted
to hold the heart together.
Or, tissue from the brain
or lungs or stomach
must be grafted across the cut.

More ordinary disappointments,
confrontations
and setbacks
also affect the heart:
the thousands of daily jabs
of electrical or adrenalin shock
leave areas of each atrium and ventrical
pockmarked or excessively spongy,
tenderer than usual
or abnormally thickened and coarse.

Such changes to the heart are clearly evident
by a person's forties.
It is common for a man or woman in that decade
to remove the heart
and examine it, noting the differences
from when he or she was younger
and attempting to account for the obvious devastation.
The battered heart sits on a cloth
in front of them, its convoluted surface a morass
of healed and half-healed
notches, slits
and contusions.
Sections of it may have gone dead
from stress or trauma,
other parts are engorged with blood

because of too-active capillaries.
Yet as the owner of the heart watches,
the organ effortlessly
contracts and
expands, apparently capable of absorbing
more
adverse treatment,
of continuing to sustain
a human life.

SANDY SHREVE

triolet
Making Love

making love with you I feel
my body wrap around the earth
a warm cocoon, content long after
making love with you. I feel
at home with everyone all day,
cannot imagine indifference after
making love. With you, I feel
my body wrap around the earth

KATE BRAID

Tool: "Instrument for Getting a Grip on the World"

Daphne Marlatt

1. *Hammer*

Hammer, you are number one/androgyne.
Don't tell
how I love your shape, long
like a man,
the ridges in your sides rubbed smooth
like a woman
by my hand.

Let me hold you close
to the callous,
guide your energy, flow of
head to nail, to wood, to waler and stud,
all of my power to drive
further
into the places I love
the best, the wood.
Drive it
home, my man/
power, woman power
mine. Yes!

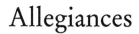

Allegiances

PHIL HALL

Lullaby

Trees creaking in the wind
To hear them you must be very still

I am walking my daughter back to sleep
(she has croup and a fever)

Feel her breathing on your neck
wind a million and one years old
    (yours a million and 36 years old)

As you walk hardwood creaks
    (trees in the wind if you're very still)

I am walking her a forest then
    in which her breath will rise
if we don't succumb to the creakings of trees

A forest will creak as she paces your ward
Wind will die in a pay-phone

Wind will rise to her full height
A floor will creak with the weight of her health

Trees are creaking in the wind
I am trying not to listen with my arms

PAM TRANFIELD

For Wynn at Two Weeks

you were not the lusty-voiced
pink child of my imagination

after thirty-eight hours
you were pulled out of me by suction
limp   gray

no time to put you
on my belly
a doctor held you while
Bill cut your cord
another doctor rushed you
across the room
to another doctor
a voice at my elbow explained
oxygen
I heard you cry   twice

Bill returned with you
for the ritual laying on the breast;
too tired to suck   you
looked into my eyes
and a nurse took you
to go upstairs   for observation
a voice explained

nine months of daydreams
reduced to fiction;
after your birth
the three of us did not sit close
under dim lights
looking at each other;
a doctor stitched my perineum
a nurse removed the epidural from my back
took blood from my arm
Bill snored in a chair beside the bed
while upstairs you were connected

to intravenous glucose
erythromycin;
I could not touch you for days.

Wynn
today you noticed the cat
reached for Bill's beard
smiled at me from my breast;
Wynn
the perfect girl
child of my dreams.

M.C. WARRIOR

for Bevan, on his first tooth

> "stranger, tell the Spartans that we lie here
> still obedient to their laws."

not that anyone now cares, Bevan.
they could have died at Hysiae,
Pylos, or Leuctra
and no one now living
could tell you the difference.
Thermopylae or Aegospotami,
to us they're nothing but some scraps
of poetry, some shards of pottery,
and a few broken columns.

so it will be in twenty-five
hundred years with you and i
and with all the quarrels
we are yet to have.
not that we'll mind,
since the dead care for nothing
except perhaps the resurrection.

yet even Leonidas, before combing
his hair for the last time
in the shade so thoughtfully
provided by Xerxes' arrows,
yes, surely even he
must have tickled his daughter's belly
or blown raspberries at his son.
if not, he died to no purpose.

one's country and one's principles
are mere abstractions, meaningless

unless made flesh and blood.

SANDY SHREVE

White Lies

Surely the child's eyes
betrayed the lie—despite
the calm assurance of words
delivered precisely the way
my father had earlier
formed them for me
(just in case we're not home,
this is what to say. . .)

But no. The census taker
hastily noted:
father, working—specific location;
number of children—sex, age;
mother, housewife—does not work.

Then left behind
her friendly smile,
subtle traces of cologne
and a child concealing
the fact of her mother's
typing at home for money,
a fact my parents feared
once ingested by any
government agency
would be smuggled through promises
of confidentiality
to income-tax inspectors
who should not know
of money coming in
unless it's going to be reported
and paid for.

This was my first lesson
in the higher education
of permissible 'little white lies'—
from which I learned
one truth about governments,
one falsehood about housewives

ZOË LANDALE

Allegiances

How our lives still touch, tie;
the hand-sewn red cloth ribbon   saved from
two Christmases ago
sewn onto a bag for drill bits.
          The man who is not your son.

All those 2 a.m. talks, *One last cigarette*
wrapped into pretty paper now;
letters, months I spend wondering
what I can afford
for your birthday.
You mail me antique jewellery;
translucent orange carnelian,
cards with miniaturized writing, half
decipherable.

          Autumn spiders.   Huge, hairy—
          There's one now!   Under your chair
          beside your foot.
          When I startled   curled toes into safety,
          the cushion,
            you'd laugh wickedly.
Did you kill them for me?
Call one of the men?

How I see you:
kitchen windows steamed with
triumphant sticky smell of citrus
surrounded by jars of Seville marmalade.
This is Phyllis' recipe, I say
twelve years of usage, a loan.
          The phone calls you make,
            special occasions.

Mother-in-law.
I always forget to say *former*. Allegiances and
  the way we speak around them.
   What we exchange; long-distance hugs,
   jaunty colours of ribbon.

PHIL HALL

Old Movies & Cheap Wine

My grandfather Wilfred Hall
was the illegitimate son of an Aldred
and a woman whose married name was Hall

She came from down near Port Perry
and soon went back there without the bastard

He was mostly known for his mouthiness
and for being a mean drunk

His first wife Mary Ryan
died when my father was 5 years old

She poisoned herself
or someone poisoned her
with wintergreen

His second wife Lizzie
was a piss-&-coal Victorian lush
with this high-pitched way of screaming
Mine! Mine!

She lived till she was 87
because she was just too damn miserable to die

At 13 my father was cutting cord-wood
with a cross-cut saw for a dollar a day

walking the 8 miles to Burnt River every Friday for groceries
bringing them home on his back to find
they hadn't even set him a place to eat at the table

He says when he finally decided to leave
he stole the only snap-shot of his real mother
intending to blow it up later
(fruit-bedecked head, puffed sleeves)

As he went out the door
my grandfather yelled after him
in the fine tradition of old movies & cheap wine
You'll be hung by the time you're 21!

By the time he was 29 and my mother was 16
they were living above the Kent Hotel in Lindsay

He was slinging beer at night
fixing and dealing old cars on the side
bootlegging to the Indians
at Curve Lake on the weekends

Every Friday old Wilf & Lizzie
would find some way into town
expecting enough of my father's cheque
for a weekend drunk

They'd get it

Then Saturday night
the old man would come back
punch-drunk
wanting to fight

& my father would hold him by the arms
till he calmed down

When he finally died
I spent an hour on the ice in the tool-shed
watching one of our hounds
eat one of her dead puppies

My mother dressed me in a little black suit
and a white silk scarf just like my father's

who lead me by hand to the edge of his father's grave

As I watched two men huff with shovels
what I thought was a sniffle
the beginning of tears high above me
when I looked up

was only my father flaring his nostrils
gritting his loose teeth and snorting

PAM TRANFIELD

Ideogram

Headlamp, root or bone? All things under earth read the same.
Trowels and gloved hands judge history carelessly so I must see
colour. Blue. No, closer to green. Medicine after the war? Or wine
enjoyed with his Sunday roast? His cow. His land. His wound.
Gifts of the government. I'm accused of having his hands so I'll
 try to be gentle finding its shape, lifting it from the earth.
The length of a newborn baby and according to depth, middle-aged.
One hand length into the earth, an underhand throw from where
was the back porch. Thrown in a drunken fit, rather than in pain or
anger; times when he acted more purposefully. This time he missed
the trees, flung sideways rather than from the neck which, if
aimed, would make a straight path toward a tree. Dirt can cover
fractures I know but this one is whole before I lift. Whole,
cold, the ground remains embossed with its shape and a language:
a human figure with a heart and running below a horse; rib bones
showing.

DAVID R. CONN

In the Granary

In the granary of my family
there is a black kernel
sifting through the bins.
I didn't know you, Grandfather.
I've never seen your grave.

Your CNR ball-peen hammer
was more real than photographs.
I put my palm to the hardwood
handle, thinking there was
nothing else of you.

That hammer lay idle
after the Toronto layoffs,
mocked you while on relief.
Shell-shocked, unemployed,
you brooded too long.

In the small hours,
a shadow passes through
the house, catching my eye:
a lost life, dark
as dead branches.

Your moods are part
of the blood that hisses
in my ears. Open the hopper,
and the bad seed comes down,
a patrimony to struggle against.

Choices

PHIL HALL

In His Name

When I have dedicated myself
to silence and death again

when I look at my hands
and think *instruments of hopelessness*

then I force my thumbs into my belt-loops
and think about Woody Guthrie
in the last years of his nervous disorder
Huntington's Chorea

his thumbs hooked into his belt-loops
by attendants
so his hands wouldn't strum in wide arcs
and break against corridor walls

I walk his derailed impulses
and try to engender within myself
his humour and conviction

I listen to him until I regain
my love of the complex squabble between
biology and gravity

all our old pre-legal hankerings for justice

solidarity with the inanimate

indignation
prickly/sweet as a gooseberry

common bush-league hellry

enough to unhook my thumbs
and close my hands into fists

or turn them into one ribbed cup
leaking light and water

or turn them into water lilies
(liquifactioning waxy gold)

—into any self-blesséd thing

enough to dedicate myself
again—in his name

to singing about what is wrong
with how we live

KIRSTEN EMMOTT

Punctum

Neruda's voice, his passion from the other side of death
brings tears to my eyes.
no one sees;
the grief of the heart
is carried away
by the lacrimal duct.

in the corner of the eye
a tiny dot sits on the eyelid;
the punctum, the mouth of the duct
whose sole purpose
is to carry away tears.

it can manage only one tear.
should Neruda speak another line
the second tear
will spill over.

The anatomy book
does not mention Neruda.
The punctum evolved
long before
the Fascists shelled Madrid.

SANDY SHREVE

Eye Contact

Days repeat themselves in a grey
weight of clouds, pressed against
her shoulders like a drenched coat.
On this street, she reflects
an absence of trees—seems only
a remote flower, a petal
sealed within a bud that spring
keeps missing

I've been striding past her
every day now, for weeks,
each time, my body taut as a thread
about to break—as if it will
if I look straight at her
smile and nod when she holds
out her hand for a quarter

I pass into the store, pretend I
do not hear her winced plea,
knowing I'll save the change
for her anyway. Will come out
head clamped to avoid her glance,
drop the silver where I expect
her palm to be.

But yesterday, she'd
curled her fingers to her coat
against the cold, and the sound
of money tickling concrete
broke my practiced trance

for an instant, our eyes met awkwardly.
Then mine sidled away like thieves
and her gaze spilled to the pavement
to capture metal seeds

CHRISTINE MICKLEWRIGHT

Smoky Mountain

The sticky heat of a Manila morning defeats the efforts of noisy electric fans as I struggle out of my net-covered dormitory bed and head for my morning rituals in the bathroom.

Breakfast stares back at me. Oily omelette, greasy sausage and cold rice. I clean my plate. Sleepy jet-lagged women grin at each other across plastic covered tables. Today we are going to Smoky Mountain. That sounds nice, I think to myself as I gather my camera and slip on my favourite pair of sandals.

We crowd onto a jeepney, a form of transport that falls somewhere between a bus and a taxi. The plastic sheeting along the side of the vehicle is rolled up so we can easily see the colour and squalor of street life in Manila.

Smoky Mountain is not a tourist area. It's a small community of many families who "process" trash. Home for these poor people is Manila's garbage dump, a hillside that oozes black mud, the stench of spoiled food and human waste.

The citizens of Smoky Mountain greet us warmly, smiling and waving. The little children stand in clusters, staring and giggling. They eagerly invite us inside their shanty houses, clean and sparse, built from corrugated iron sheets, discarded plywood and bedsprings. There are even little tea shops at the top of the mountain where the locals relax, gossiping over cakes and beverages.

The recent rains have drenched the site and the black putrid mud climbs over the top of my sandals as I pick my way across the clutter. Hundreds of people are sorting through the newly arrived waste, retrieving bottles, cloth, plastic, and other items tossed out by those who consider them useless rubbish. Bulldozers clamber around the top of the mountain, burying the unusable refuse. The Smoky Mountain residents clean, wash, polish, and mend every possible item, then go back out on to the streets of the city, hawking their wares.

Women with soap-covered hands are squeezing and wringing laundry in plastic buckets, hanging the clean ragged garments on clotheslines stretched between the shanties. Skinny cats exist on the few scraps that fall from the hands of children, and chase the rats and mice that scavenge over the site.

I pause at one of the many patchwork houses. A gnarled old man stands behind a fence of twisted bedsprings and rusted corrugated iron sheets. His eyes squint in the sun. Gray haired, with the stubble of a beard on his bony face, he beckons me. I hesitate. The bus driver urges me forward.

A young girl with shiny black eyes and long ebony hair skips out from the house, clutching a small rag doll. Her hand-me-down dress is neatly patched and perfectly white. Her round pixie face stares up at me. I crouch down to her level, looking straight into her beautiful eyes. She hesitates, shifts her feet, glancing to the ground, then suddenly launches herself at me. Her arms grasp tightly around my neck and I feel the surprising wetness of her tears spilling against my face.

The old man speaks rapidly to the bus driver who turns to me. "His granddaughter lost her mother last year. There is no money to look after the children. He asks you . . . please take her with you. Give her a life she cannot have here."

The little girl holds me tight. I feel overwhelmed. An impossible request. Slowly, regretfully, I disentangle the young girl's arms from around my neck. I wipe the tears from her face and gently, sadly shake my head.

From my bag I retrieve a pale green ballpoint pen. In large letters it declares "Hawaii", my own souvenir of a recent visit. I press it into the young girl's hand. She takes it, examining it closely. Then she looks up at me as I rise to my feet. She smiles. The biggest, widest smile. I grin back at her, ruffle her hair softly and turn away feeling a small ache in my chest.

We wave goodbye, board our jeepney and rumble through the dirty, crowded streets. Within minutes we are comfortably settled in a lush green park, the site of Fort Santiago, built by the Spanish.

In the clean public washroom I flush my badly stained feet under a cool gushing tap. My sandals hang stiffly in my hand, filthy and ruined. At the end of the day I will toss them in the garbage, bidding them farewell as they journey back to Smoky Mountain.

TOM WAYMAN

Sure, I Was Paid Well

but the money felt
like a thick stack of bills
had been folded once and crammed in my open mouth

so what I wanted to say
was blocked, or at the very least garbled
by the wad of dollars

         and my jaws ached
with the strain of being held apart
by the cash. Though I tried to dress well

I wasn't sure if people on the street
mocked me behind my back
for being so funny-looking

with a mouth stuffed with currency.
Or maybe they didn't see me at all
but only saw the clump of bills

that pressed down on my tongue.
When I sought out others paid as much as me
I found myself calculating how thick

their gag of dollars was
compared to mine. In any case
it was difficult to talk about the experience we had in common

since their words were hard to distinguish
through the money. And I confess
I was afraid to stick my fingers in behind

and lever the currency out; I was fearful of
what was dammed up
behind that cash,

of what the absence of those dollars
would release. And I was anxious
that the wad of money

would turn out to be an illusion:
a few genuine bills on the outside of the roll
and the rest only paper,

paper.

SANDY SHREVE

Whiter than White

this paper is poison
a flat sheet of foolscap
bleached to a concept of cleanliness
fit to kill

its afterbirth bloats rivers and seas
leaches into salmon and seals
turns up in mothers' milk

and milk cartons
made cleaner than clean
the way we're supposed to keep
household ingredients—sheets, shirts,
floors, toilets, tubs
we scrub scrub scrub
flush chemical misconceptions
down the drain

the message assaults our senses:
everything has to be white
including neighbours
colours must sparkle and sheen
like the whiter than whites
compete with pristine northern snow
where an Inuit child suckles dioxins

miles from their origins
in this white-obsessed world
whose palest-skinned race
blanched of pigment
names itself universal
flesh coloured

where clean is considered
immaculately white
and we finger particles of power
that dissolve to death

GLEN DOWNIE

Skywriting

Driving the long night highways, I search out a song
to steer by. There is no star, not even our victim
moon. Trucks transporting missiles threaten
to overtake me. I can hear
the song that guides them;
it is not a love song.

In the small hours of dawn, the clouds collapse
and weep in the harrowed fields. There is a scar
on the morning—skywriting
coming undone. This is a dead zone
on the radio. I take up
my father's driving song: a spiritual
I haven't sung for years.

ZOE LANDALE

Poison on the Wind

Based on a series from *The Christian Science Monitor*

Lament of the Bulldozers

If I tell you these bodies had birthdays
would that peel them upright from photographs
make them as real as you, eating popcorn?
From the flat symbolism of statistics,
I have walked into their horror
God, they have *eyes*   they wear shirts
with buttons   the living drink water
from cups, they are not, I tell you
television ghosts   zzzip on and psst off
the bodies stink   they need to be disposed
of quickly, with ululations of bull-dozers
And water-drinking relatives
stretch out grieving burnt hands to the shirts with
buttons and the statistics who fill them
limp   Did I mention there are animals, too?
Donkeys and cows, their ears in such unnatural,
stick-out shapes, not flapping at flies
in the 115 degree heat

It comforts me you are safe
I need comfort
You and our girl at home
sitting in the big brown chair
eating popcorn
Newspaper fanned around
the hand-made rag rug your aunt gave us
for Christmas
white on rose on red on rust
You flap a page in air
our girl jabs the other side
What's that?
Giant worms from New Zealand, you say
turning the paper over

worms the size of garter snakes
Should we get some for our garden?
No way, she says
has a drink of her sparkling water
and lime cordial
Is my birthday soon?

Career-Oriented

No worries, isn't that what we want, most of us?
Enough money, a bit more
than we have now, always that edge of comfort
or smoothness which recedes
Harmless enough
and thiodiglycol is also a wetting
agent in the manufacture of inks
for ballpoint pens, that must be
what Iraq wanted 500 metric tons of it for,
Phillips Petroleum (Belgium) must have
thought so, right?
If they thought
The order was on paper
no bodies convulsed and died on the sleek
grey carpet releasing sphincters
smelling vilely human and inconveniencing visitors
at the front entrance
profit is the Name
all the papers were in order

Introducing:
THIODIGLYCOL   a versatile product
with a good balance
of properties and applications
water white
practically odourless
high purity
low oral toxicity
reacts like a typical glycol
a precursor to mustard gas
Get all the facts on new THIODIGLYCOL
Call 312-807-3273

Halabja, the dead city
I think about money often, it's like
icy lemonade   infinitely desirable in the heat
and like imaginary lemonade
I can't taste   I can't touch
sweat on the moustaches of the men
who profit from these nerve agents
and chemical precursors
I watch their navy-blue suits
march confidently up watered lawns
faces blobs
of flesh-coloured plasticine
They don't kick dogs, cats or torture their
children   Some are gourmet cooks
Their wives are traditional, head committees
wish their men
would spend more time with their families

I have been in Samarra when
it was operating
If it were making nerve gas
I would be dead
> Bernd Hermann, chief representative of Karl Kolb
> & Co in Iran, West German manufacturers

Countless tons of nerve agents
have been produced in plants
without the death of the
operators or other inside
Until they are mixed,
they act like other industrial
chemicals
> Expert consultant to the U.S. government

We do not supply things
for chemical warfare
> William Shammas, Baghdad representative of Karl
> Kolb in Iran

There's quite an elaborate
infrastructure worldwide
involved in actively camou-
flaging suspect transactions
                    U.S. official

Some must be women
with thin black briefcases
though their faces too are only ovals
I see the ovals as owls
white   hardly believable
floating silently above the sidewalk at dusk

Exchange

When the mail clatters through the slot
in the front door,
our girl runs to get it
Can I open this one? she asks
And this?

The rule is exchange, she has to pick up shreds
of envelopes left behind
Legs straight out in front of her on the floor,
she laughs   ripping paper
Last year, the U.S. government had to stop
sending biological agents to defense labs
through the mail
After public protest
the government now uses private couriers
such as Federal Express
The labels have a warning symbol on them;
they use waterproof tape on the packages

Microbe alert:
in an aerosol attack
less than 1 ounce of tularemia bacteria
produces a cloud higher than a 20-storey
building and .62 miles wide,
emits thousands of infection doses per minute
The Pentagon has acknowledged
they are researching military uses of:
Yersina pestis,

remember "Black Death"?
Yellow fever we all know, and polio
Anthrax
The O'Nyong Nyong virus is an exotic
Toxin from cobras
Mojave desert rattlesnakes
scorpions
shellfish
Gene-splicing means cheap toxicity;
in one day a single cell makes
281 trillion copies of itself
What scares sensible scientists
is the possibility of *novel agents*
eerie fusion between bacteria
viruses and toxins
And we thought AIDS was bad?
What about plague, improved
since the fourteenth century when
25 million people died from it in Europe?
Begin with a wildly infectious fever
which when treated suddenly begins to resemble
poisoning by snake venom
which when treated   kills the patient
Help! Vaccines!
We must experiment further in case
The Others   develop such a weapon
in the course of their also
purely defensive research
Except   what if someone succeeds
in creating a mutation with   no cure?

These Scientists

Anthrax Island, as the locals call it,
or Gruinard Island, off the coast of Scotland
has finally been decontaminated after
46 years
Formaldehyde and sea water applied through
miles of drip hoses
cleaned up the migration of anthrax spores
under the soil;

linked fila-forms of tough gossamer
microbe art
successful beyond the 1941 scientists' maddest
expectations
They just wanted to explode containers of anthrax spores
watch a few tethered sheep die
and take notes on how fast

Nerve agent Tabun GA smells of fruit and is fatal
An apple blossom smell or pepper
lets the victim know they're under the influence
of an incapacitating agent
Phosgene will choke a person to death
on the smell of new-mown hay
These scientists think of everything

Once in a Land Far Far Away

What of the men in their navy-blue suits
the women with black briefcases,
their worries at tax time
the casual disavowal they practice
toward responsibility?
Not their concern what happens to the stuff
they just make chemicals
trade
sell
buy

The strategic payload of one bomber
is 15 tons of nerve gas
The noise of rupturing lungs
is in a foreign language
doesn't carry as far
as the air-conditioned offices, the green lawns

In Halabja, the desolate city
the rigid fingers of those unnumbered dead
say: What would it take?
A locket from a child's blistered neck
to the secretary who processed the thiodiglycol
order? The child will not rub it
for comfort again

A package, delivered late at night
to one of the warehousemen who shipped the chemical,
a photograph of a smiling young couple
attached to a red sock with
a foot still inside?
A grandmother's scarf to a black-briefcase woman
the cotton enclosing two arms, upraised
as though in prayer? Surely the woman
would understand the old arms
in her immaculate tile entryway
spoke the language of common humanness
of chopping vegetables for dinner
of waking into cool dawns and gladness
at the smell of cooking food,
the solidity of a small child nestled
in one's arms

Artisan

I think of you
in the brown chair, newspaper strewn about,
and I miss you
There's something wrong with my tummy,
our daughter says, so solemn
It needs kisses
Her half-moon warmth smells of good West German
soap, a green frog
we put in her Christmas stocking
Give our girl a hug
I'm still tracing profiles of predators
who they hold dear
who waits for them at night,
A Burmese cat, a family?
I work with paper too
Behind every casualty figure is the person
it represents
a widow's peak of blonde hair, say
or the tender hollow of a teenager's throat
From paper I want to broadcast an incurable infection
of real people
all the easy-to-put-aside newspaper photographs

metastasizing
to fly-blown dead eyes of
I   me   mine

PAM TRANFIELD

Dreams

on our first walk after your birth
we passed an old man
he looked into your carriage
good looking boy he said
I told him you are a girl
dressed in blue today,
he said he had six daughters
and that if he had a gun
he would shoot them all

last night you slept
through the screams of a woman
attacked outside our building;
you woke in the morning
laughing

today in Value Village
a four year old boy
walked up to you
with a plastic gun aimed
I yelled "no"
he ran crying
into the arms
of his mother.

daughter
I cannot protect you forever;
boys grow into men
live out their fantasies;
a month before your birth
fourteen students were murdered
shot
because they were women;
some day
you will know this,
some day you will face
a man on the bus

eyes/hands all over you,
you will walk necessary streets
at night
aware of shadows
the speed of a passing car

but in this sweet short time
night is for sleep
and tonight I am close;
sleep daughter
grow strong
strong for the day when
you will need more than a smile
to dissolve the darkness.

KIRSTEN EMMOTT

A Difficult Birth

William Chamberlen invented the forceps,
kept them hidden from the midwives,
taught their use to his sons only
as women struggled and died unaided;
for one hundred years
until the secret leaked out
the Chamberlens bragged
they could deliver anyone,
charged high fees,
carried the bag in with great show,
lifted out the mysterious implements
unseen, worked covered with a sheet,
put them away unseen;

the king's dwarf lay in labour,
she had been in labour for days,
many midwives had tried and failed.
Peter Chamberlen was summoned,
he struggled for three hours
before admitting defeat.
She must have been quite young, let us say fifteen,
possibly a rape victim,
she was in pain,
did not know what was being done to her,
she died in agony.

Her name
has not come down to us.

SANDY SHREVE

Abortion

Prepped
jabbed
anaesthetized—
the saline chill
prickles its way
through my veins

My womb
one more piece
in the hospital's
monotonous
assembly line,
soon scraped clean
of the thrill
to feel
I am pregnant!
Of the fears—
how could I
raise a child
alone and poorly paid,
scraped with the same
bored precision
as are fish
when gutted
for freezing.

Discharged,
clutching the cold
religious pamphlets
birth control handbooks
and accusing eyes,
I march
with pro-choice parades
knowing even they
can't make necessity
easy

CHRISTINE MICKLEWRIGHT

Choices—To Have or To Have Not

They've called a Commission
　　of the Royal kind
　　to inquire, to report
　　on reproductive
　　technology
　　and they say
　　they have a MANdate.

They aren't shy,
　　they ask all:
　　ownership of
　　ova, sperm, embryos
　　and foetal tissue
　　A probe really,
　　supposed to be painless
　　extracting the personal
　　to couch in the political.

Infertility, surrogate,
　　sterilization, insemination,
　　consent;
　　choose a boy
　　or maybe a girl
　　order a genius
　　and pay the price
　　to those who hold
　　a patent
　　of the perfect type,
　　the commercial hype
　　if we allow it.

What have they ever cared
　　about workplace struggles?
　　unhealthy
　　and damaging
　　conditions
　　which create fear

for the unborn
and those
that will never be
or those flawed on arrival.

Money can rent wombs
buy babies,
sign up for the impossible
the famous in-vitro
only seven per cent successful,
and the average working woman
learns
that medicare won't pay.

Choice is always our issue
it never changes
while privatization
and legislation
limit choices.
The child I can not have
the child she will not have
the child she must have.
The control must be
for us, not them
health costs within our means
and childcare in reach
of working mothers, working poor.

The laboratories hum
as donated embryos
grow and form
shaped by unknown hands
in unknown agendas
destined for unknown futures;
experimentation,
for whose benefit?
It could be mine
it could be yours
Make it our choice.

Ethics and morals
religion and conscience
heartache and dilemmas

some facing
childlessness
others denied
abortions
while those who can
pour money into test tubes
hopes and dreams
meeting disappointments.

I stare at my VDT
humming at 60 cycles
fingers caressing keys
eyes scanning screens
breathing fumes
squinting under fluorescent
lunch in the microwave
ozone around the copier
filters on the taps
ammonia in the washroom;
some handle heavy freight
and dangerous goods
working shifts
midnights and dawns
while happy pregnant women
come and go
come and go
most seem lucky
but the sad stories sit quietly
and we only wonder
but never really know
why her child is like that
why she can't get pregnant
why she miscarries.

And the Commission
will barely give us a day
to tell those stories
of grief and hope
asking for choices
asking for care
asking for regulation
for medicare

for safe work
for wishes and dreams
for that happy family life
in whatever way we choose
for ourselves.

KIRSTEN EMMOTT

Bread

LADY   ME *lavedi*, OE *hlafdige*, ?orig. meaning loaf-kneader
equiv. to *hlaf* loaf + *dige* var. of *daige* kneader (see
DOUGH) compare Icelandic *deigja* maiden

The artists now are making giant displays
in homage to women's arts:
china painting, needlework, quilting.
Wait till they find out about bread!
Always a women's art, needed but not noticed,
ephemeral, consumed, thrown out if not fresh,
each loaf the work of hours;
an apprenticeship of years is required,
the novice beside her mother,
kneading the dough.

The yeast is brought from its sleep when sprinkled on the water,
the warm water tested like a baby's bath,
not too hot, not too cold,
so that a bowl of foam is ready for the flour;
then the loaf, a living thing,
slowly changing under the kneading hands,
letting go of the sticky board and gathering itself together.

A loaf will change visibly as you watch,
it becomes playful, bounces this way and that,
and then lies coiled and waiting
rebounding from the finger.
It swells silently on the window sill
beside the flat stiff layers of the piecrust.

I lift the mass of dough and tilt it back and forth.
Shape it—it shapes itself back into a ball.
It seems the same size and weight as a premature baby.
It grows, however, more quickly.
I sometimes think of the children upstairs
as rising slowly in their beds like loaves.

This confuses me, as they are not intended
for consumption.

In a cool kitchen the yeast will not rise.
Warm the kitchen,
not too hot or the yeast will die.
When the loaves are plump,
put them into the hot oven.
The yeast must love the heat at first,
frantically dividing as they die.
So do many uprisings fail,
with only bubbles produced
to raise someone else's bread.

SANDY SHREVE

Taking Back the Night

A woman, alone at a window
shudders as she watches
the dark outside

House after house it's the same.
Separately framed, hands
clench sills.

The hour has reverted
to an early dark—
each of us, last Sunday morning
got up, obedient, fingered
our own clocks back
to standard time

no time now for that
after dinner stroll
when we could breathe in the hush
of early evening air. Already
it's night, and so far
only our slogan
has retrieved it from fear

So far, instead of walking
we rage inside
and stare

Neighbours

SANDY SHREVE

Neighbours

We discover each other slowly, through
summer afternoons renovating our houses—
hear histories between hammer strokes
about whose place used to be whose
or the school behind the transit line
once a dairy farm
our urban lots the hayfield
until it burned

newcomers and oldtimers are introduced
grow comfortable with people
who never would have cared to meet
if they hadn't chanced on the same block

we say the same about most relatives,
co-workers; if not for blood
or job ties, we'd have nothing in common
let the comment pass as if it's a given
as if proof exists in how easily we lose touch
when we move on
though they change us forever
and we them

A citied-in street slows
the hurry-home from errands
with the syrup of blackberry scent and sweet peas
urging us back toward something
of the country town:
a craving for everyone to know everyone,
what we've been up to

Fences eventually become supports to lean words on
porches a reason to pause
as we become neighbours for a season
stitching together the remnants of a village
before winter sets in

M.C. WARRIOR

where there's muck,
there's brass

"what Manchester thinks today
the world will think tomorrow."
—Industrial Revolution proverb

Grimsby, Yarmouth, Bradford,
Rochdale, Wigan, Salford,
Huddersfield, Middlesborough, Leeds

names which fall from the tongue
like scars. names which echo
in the memory like Nineveh and Babylon.
names which make an exile wish
he could sit down by the waters
of the Fraser and weep.

Bradford, Leeds, Rochdale,
Sheffield, Middlesborough, Wigan,
Yarmouth, Grimsby, Salford

like the regimental standards
of a forgotten army, these names
speak of battles lost: of sleet
and grime and clogs
clacking up road to mill
in the murk of morning's gas light.

Salford, Huddersfield, Grimsby,
Wigan, Leeds, Sheffield,
Rochdale, Hinderwell, Bradford

names which once turned
the world upside-down,
which overthrew Czars,
Kaisers, and Buonapartes,
which built libraries, museums,
and galleries called, not

after our Tom, Dick, and Elsie,
but after Krupp, Rockefeller,
and Carnegie. the names of the cities
whose workers built the modern world,
and which, thirty years ago,
were still my home.

Grimsby, Manchester, Leeds,
Wigan, Huddersfield, Blackpool,
Sheffield, Rochdale, Bradford

no longer use the bricks we'll use
to build the New Jerusalem

no more a target
for the arrows of desire

nowt left here
to live and die for

but signposts
on the high road to Liverpool,
that toll road to Montreal,
Buenos Aires, or Sydney,
the cart track to anywhere
but the place i was born, an exile.

TOM WAYMAN

They Made My City into Two Cities

Vancouver

They made my city into two cities
I was watching but they did it anyway
One city with the sea breeze pouring up
through the clean streets
shadowed by enormous chestnut and cedar trees
under which are expensive boutiques and restaurants
houses costing so much you feel unworthy just looking at them
And down at the harbour, marinas full of boats priced
almost as high as the houses
with pennants flying gaily from masts
and from the balconies of taverns, import shops
and even food markets
catering exclusively to the rich
And to the east
is the other city
sidewalks cracked and patched
the trees spindly, discount merchandise for sale
and no ocean
except an industrial waterfront
vigilantly protected by the Ports police:
grain elevators, fish canneries, warehouses
with fences and railroad yards to keep you
as distant as possible from what might have been beaches
The avenues are stifling, if it isn't raining
the bars jammed and smoky
and, outside, the buses drag us from place to place
looking for work, like defective goods
being offered as joblots to various junk dealers
Even the mountains to the north, that on the west side
sparkle beautifully
here look vaguely menacing, like a health care premium increase
or a cut in welfare
The massive peaks seem like duties or procedures

we're going to have to fulfill
to stay out of jail

Wait a minute, I can hear you saying
Weren't there always two cities?
And who are the "they" you're blaming
again for the world's troubles?

Yes, there were always two cities: the wealthy and the poor
But I grew up here, and don't remember
the gap so large
I don't recall businesses like the take-out Italian restaurant
that announced they would not deliver east of Main
or the monthly magazine issued by the largest newspaper
distributed only to the western half of my city
(You should have read the paper's consumer columnist
justifying this—how we'd all benefit
since the increased revenues would result in an improved daily
    product
even for east enders, blah blah blah)
There was certainly a ritzy neighbourhood or two
but I don't remember the quarantining of so many districts
to eliminate anyone not rolling in money
as inflated house prices result
in only a tiny percentage of human beings
being able to live there
I don't remember this situation
encouraging real estate profiteers
to demolish what cheaper dwellings survive in every neighbourhood
and to replace them with staggeringly expensive apartments and
    homes
I know a swath was never cut through the east side
to build a little toy elevated train
to deliver we slaves to our downtown jobs faster
(since house costs have forced us to live further and further from
    work)
Somebody kept insisting how wonderful this elevated system
was going to be, though they had to trash the bus service
to get enough of us to ride on it
to justify its existence
and a special tax had to be added onto both gasoline
and our electricity bill

to help subsidize such a marvel
Best of all were the cries of outrage
that went up from the west side
when it was proposed that the little train should cut through
their neighbourhoods
to connect with a suburb to the south into which
more of us had been pushed
"Not on your life!" the howl went up.
"Who do you think we are? *Who*
do you think we are?"

And that question brings us to your other point:
who *are* the "they"
that tore my city into two
(and who, as far as I can tell,
would be happy if they could eradicate the poorer half entirely
leaving this place restricted to the well-heeled)?
This is a question that's bothered me most of my life:
who decided that those who own an enterprise
should get more money than the rest of us who work at it each day?
I'm not talking about the wage structure, understand
I know each of us can construct dozens of excuses
why we should be paid more than the women or men working
    alongside us
No problem there (though this is what helps keep
the majority of us earning a lot less than we could be)
I'm talking about *decisions*: who, and how was it, determined
my city should be two cities?

Some people blame it on offshore money:
Japanese yen with nowhere else to be spent
Hong Kong dollars that have to be extracted from the colony
before the Chinese government at last reclaims
what belongs to its people
On the east side, graffiti expresses this viewpoint
with the area's usual delicate regard for personal feelings:
"Chinks hired? You're fired!"
the walls say. On the west side, the matter
is handled a little differently
such as when the federal government gave the Bank of Hong Kong
five million dollars "to financially assist"
their purchase of the Bank of B.C.

Such solidarity among the wealthy
—sharing around the trough of public money
for their own profit—regardless of skin colour
or national origin
maybe expresses a healthier outlook, however,
than ours
For aren't we all immigrants
except for the tribes we hurt so viciously?
How can we draw a line and say:
"Now that I'm here, everybody else who arrives
is an alien life form"?
In any case, for every overseas arrival who buys in
somebody local must have sold out
Are the latter folks, then, the elusive "they"
I want to blame?
I observe how men and women from the other city
keep showing up where we live
to try to talk land prices higher and higher
and to convince people to open upscale catering enterprises
only a few blocks from the Food Bank lines
Probably the next step will be to operate charter bus tours
to bring tourists to watch our frenzies on Cheque Day
which some west siders like to regard as
a sort of Carnival
and which I'm sure the provincial Ministry of Tourism
would like to see expanded
into parades, floats, street dances
a monthly Mardi Gras
instead of shouting and glass breaking in the street
tires screeching, people staggering blankly around
or being sick on the sidewalk
falling down, or lurching past bleeding
from a skinned forehead and cut knuckles
or with eyes blackened and a broken nose
being hauled into wagons by the cops
or directed by social workers to an already-full women's shelter

Now if you think we're not getting too far
in determining who so transformed my city
maybe I can rephrase the issue:

why should there be some men and women with too much money
and others with not enough?
Why isn't wealth, in a rich province
shared more equally? Can't we figure out
how to redistribute what we all help earn
or is it that we don't want to?
Anyway, why should the gulf between the cities
get wider and wider? Where do we go
if we can't afford to live in our neighbourhood any longer?
Why should we have to leave?

Gee, this is like a quiz
Twenty-five points for each right answer!
And if nobody can come up with the correct response
I'll finish with a few additional questions:

what's wrong with there being one city of the very well off
and one of the increasingly poor?
Who has the power to change it?
Who *should* have the power to change it?
How do we stop
what's happening to us?

SANDY SHREVE

Low Level

Imagine a few thousand of these shocks
a season:
out of nowhere
familiar sounds of the day or night
overflown
low
loud

like the shattering boom
he treated us to last year—
that airforce flyer denounced
'hot dogger'—plane-crazed kid
buzz-bombing the North Shore
caught, of course, in the act
that snatched a lot of hearts
close to attacks,
probably got grounded years
for the show-off stage

He could have gone to Nitassinan
and done it with impunity. No city
school-kids, hospital patients, office
executives etc. there to scare,
only Innu and animals

But. He didn't—took his toy jet
fighter to what we consider
a populated place. So I like to think
maybe he wasn't a hot dog after all,
but a rebel. Took up his plane
like a pen, and brought the impact down
on our heads
so we couldn't ignore it, so when
we read the papers' slight stories
on the Innu protests

we might begin to hear

GLEN DOWNIE

City Council Grapples with the Housing Crisis

They haggle in council over whether it shall be legal to burrow a hole in the ground and sleep on a leaf. And if so, how much the city can tax the owner of the land for *improvements*. Sleep on a stone, sleep on a leaf—wherever there is sleep, there are taxes and regulations. Regulations on the size of the stone, the number of sleepers on each leaf. Because every leaf and stone owes something to council. Because no one may sleep in the clutch of this city without answering to council for the width of their burrow, the length of their leaf, the depth of their sleep. And council is happy if neighbour should turn against neighbour and make an anonymous phone call saying *A man is sleeping on a leaf in my neighbour's back yard*. Then council can rub its itchy palms at the thought of another tax. Which shall it be? The tax on unauthorized leaves? Or the tax on sleeping? The tax on homeless men in back yards? And even if the leaf were legalized, there would be taxes and regulations. Tax on the business use of the leaf; regulations that it fit the neighbourhood character, that it be made of genuine leaf materials, to the approved leaf plan. Because council must be the master of all that sleeps in this, our city. Reserving for itself, of course, the freedom to sell the city outright to corporations with monstrous sleep requirements, whose home cities have long ago been twisted by the nightmares of corporate sleeping. Oh yes, a corporation may purchase all our leaves to sleep on because we have nothing but trees and leaves to sell, and there's nothing we want but money.

Incantation to Change Our Lives

TOM WAYMAN

Adult Education

A house
is the sum of the trades that construct it:
the plumber's apprentice who installs vents
and clean-out pipes
amid the studding,
while an electrician figures
where the box and wall plugs
should be placed.

        Afterwards
a woman or man
attempts to market the building
—somebody who knows how to talk,
to turn on all the lights
so the rooms seem brighter,
to arrange financing:
words
and tricks
and money.

    There are individuals
    who understand a car with water in the oil
    has a leak in the head gasket,
    while oil in the water
    means a cracked block. Other men and women
    assemble vehicles.
    And again, there are salespeople.

A society, too,
has its functioning parts.
But there is a difference between
how a machine or dwelling is viewed
by a person with a hand in its making
or repair
and someone who offers it for sale.

Those who claim to speak on our behalf:
are they builders
or sellers? What have they planned
to do with our lives?

M.C. WARRIOR

the world turned upside down

this is an incendiary,
a subversive,
a chain poem.

each worker who reads it,
each typist, each carpenter,
each nurse, each millworker,
must pass it on
to their fellow workers
or the chain will be broken.

everyone of you who reads
this poem must also write
a poem of your own,
or the chain will be broken.

do not show your poem
to anyone else—it is yours,
for yourself, alone.

it is a hard poem
i ask of you—
harder to confront
than a bank manager,
than a father refusing
to pay child support.

i ask that you write
about the eight hours
which are the fulcrum
and the curse of your life.

as you write you will notice
that the person beside you,
the fellow worker who gave you
a copy of this poem

has left their workplace
(the coffee whistle has not sounded)

is running toward the supervisor's office
(nothing is broken down)
is putting a match to this poem
(it is not dark; the fuses are not blown)
and is hurling it through the door.

all through the plant/office/mill
a fiery glow is spreading.
over there a foreman
is clambering through a window,
down the aisle a manager
is running shoeless to the street.

their world is on fire.
so far no one has reached
for an extinguisher.

the chain is unbroken.

KATE BRAID

Auntie

for Kelly Pryde and Kathleen Coates

In dreams I draw my finger
over your dusty welding rods
forbidden since the war
when they said married women
can't do men's work
any more,
should be home minding babies,
sewing smocks for new citizens.
A woman's place, you always said,
was where she wanted to be.
That was the war we all lost

that time.

PAM TRANFIELD

anarchy/sisters

At 4:00 a.m. Sept. 21, 1987 three women from Yellow
Gate, Greenham Women's Peace Camp in Berkshire,
England were arrested inside the Convoy Deployment
Site on Salsbury Plain. The women were arrested after
reaching the site on foot across open plain and avoiding
high security patrols, flare wires and barbed wire rolls.
Part 1 of this poem is from a letter written by one of the
women, Sheila Tranfield, to her sister.

1.

on this early morning we parted the wire (3
coils) and climbed through
into the wood where the convoy
was loudest
Katrina   fearless
led us over wire, fallen trees
to where the launchers were hidden
in camouflage

suddenly   a head
popped out of a hole
it was wearing a helmet
covered in leaves   its face
painted green   its eyes
bright blue
we stopped
facing a machine gun
we raised our hands   saying
non violent women
and started singing
"Bella Ciao"

we moved as ordered
toward an erect launcher
two blue lights blinking

and were led to a road singing
"We are the Witches"

in the jeep   we saw
a deer on the road
hacked in two pieces

2.

sister   never the same name twice
on your letters,
records of jailhouses
names of women
women's songs
i worry about infertility   you
annihilation

sister   the daughters i have will be fearless
the first
i will name for you
and she shall sing

M.C. WARRIOR

cleaning up history

i am raising a subscription
to erect a statue
to the unknown janitor—

to the slave wiping the blood
from the republic's marble walls
while Marcus Antonius praises
his good friend Caesar.

it will be a monument
to the rest of us,
to those who must follow,
armed with mops and buckets,
after the great men of history
have tracked their muddy boots
across the kitchen floors of our lives.

no expense will be spared; this memorial
will be stronger than the wrath of heroes,
more durable than the tantrums of kings.

not even the most sycophantic
of scholars will be able
to ignore this concrete proof
that history itself requires
a regular spring cleaning.

ZOË LANDALE

Incantation to change our lives

make us smaller
a leaf or an apple
the complete way they loom
more of, perfect, mass changed
by water and root alchemy
from coiled promise to October,
Cox's Orange ripening yellow red
double-ended leaves;
festival of stemmed boats

make us
beings fastidious for a larger skin
defined as we are
by hands rising
with things wadded up inside
throwing in rivers
idealism we gave up as too painful
or gauche
diapers which fester on the barrens
for four hundred years;
we see one another in the supermarket
arms swathed in plastic
clear, with red script we neglect to decipher
our eyes fall into forgetfulness
automatism of greed

make our longings sweeter,
fill them with shapes
of trees,
not temptation in shop windows
Oriental rugs in lustrous colours,
black cursive of patterns which would look
so fine   in our worn rooms
sumptuous displays behind glass

supple leathers that suddenly,
we almost   can't do without
as the bus we are riding lurches on
we want to cry out
our hands had already closed
around those satchels
we could smell the leather, feel the heaviness

make us quiet enough
to enter into shapes of boats
with hands
neither anxious for
nor disgusted by
what we hold or do not
teach our fingers
to mould in giving,
dense and succulent as apples
matured by frost
make us over
so we serve green-shaped air,
the living community
without the bending rot   of shame

GLEN DOWNIE

Day of Singing

It begins like any other. We hear nothing stirring
in the caved-in corridors of the dark. Morning
is shower, shave, coffee. Season is umbrella
or not. The time at the tone is
standard or a false saving
of light. We have hidden from ourselves
even the cicada's intuition of something other
than this, a way out and a reason
to take it. We trust what we touch:
shoe leather, calculator, paper
mate, hard copy. Buried
since birth, he yet feels
his untried wings, and though
to live in the grave is to fear no enemies,
still some instinctual dawn breaks underground.
We meet in a windowless room
to bicker and drink rough coffee while wishing
for clearer departmental objectives. The cicada
has sustained himself these seventeen years
on root sap and an insect dream
of the day of singing. But how can we live
on four per cent when one
cancer in the steno pool eats up our relief
for the fiscal year? When he fills the trees
with the din of his mating song, he celebrates
the possible. If we could hear, we too
could come out alive. We could use the emergency
exits, stop in the NO STOPPING zone, lift
our pale, xeroxed faces to the sun. Tremulous
in the radiant day, unsure of our strength,
we could become, after years entombed,
flying men and women, beating our arms, struggling
upward over the trees, awkward at first
but aloft, our glasses and pagers, car keys and
pocket silver raining musically down as we whoop
and cry, hearts swollen, almost bursting
with joy.

BIOGRAPHICAL NOTES

Kate Braid was born in Calgary in 1947. After years of unhappy labour as a clerical and childcare worker, she stumbled onto a construction site in 1977 and has been labouring (mostly) happily ever since as a journey carpenter. In 1986 she joined VIWU and began to take writing seriously, mostly as an outlet for questions about being a woman in the trades. In 1990 she prepared a one hour radio program on women in trades for CBC's "Ideas." Published work includes nonfiction articles and poems that have appeared in magazines, literary journals and anthologies in Canada and the U.S. A collection of her poems will be published by Polestar Press this year.

David R. Conn (b. 1950) is a founding member of VIWU. During the 1970s, he spent four years working at shipbuilding and steel fabrication in Vancouver. His poetry has appeared in a number of magazines and anthologies. His chapbooks, *Harbour Light* and *Ticket Stubs for the Bullgang*, are both about the local waterfront. Since 1981, David has worked as a librarian and freelance magazine writer, covering marine topics among many others.

Glen Downie was born in Winnipeg and now lives in Vancouver, where he works with cancer patients and their families. He joined VIWU in 1984. His publications include a poem-sequence *The Blessing* (Pierian Press, 1986) and two full-length collections, *An X-Ray of Longing* (Polestar Press, 1987) and *Heartland* (Mosaic Press, 1990). A new book of poems, *The Angel of Irrational Numbers,* is expected from Press Porcépic this year.

Kirsten Emmott lives in Vancouver, where she works as a family doctor. Her poetry has appeared in numerous literary and medical periodicals and in ten anthologies. She has been a member of VIWU since 1979. *"The best thing about the field of medicine is the endless flow of interesting work to do."—Richard Gordon*

Phil Hall (b. 1953) expatriated to Vancouver from Ontario in 1979 and was welcomed as an immigrant/fellow traveller by VIWU in 1981. He helped establish the Union's "Work to Write" series in 1982. He returned to Toronto in 1985, where he currently teaches Working Class Literature for the Metro Labour Council, writes for *Books in Canada,* and edits *Don't Quit Yr Day-Job,* a labour arts magazine. He has published six books, three chapbooks, and a cassette. His most recent publications are *Amanuensis* (Brick Books, 1989) and *Pay Dirt* (songs, poems, and jazz, with Cam Young). He is currently serving as Short Term Writer-in-Residence at the University of Western Ontario.

Zoë Landale was born in 1952 and has lived most of her life in B.C. She fished commercially for seven years and wrote about it in her first book, *Harvest of Salmon* (Hancock House). Landale is now a parent, a freelance journalist, and in the time remaining, writes poetry and children's stories. Her poetry has been published in numerous journals. *Colour of Winter Air*, a book of poems, was published by Sono Nis Press. She has been a member of VIWU since 1979.

Christine Micklewright is employed as an airline passenger agent, is a Vice-President of CAW Local 1990, Vice-President of the BC Federation of Labour and a former Vice-President of the Canadian Association of Labour Media. She is a member of the New Directions collective, a columnist for Solinet, CUPE's electronic network, and has edited a union newspaper for 15 years. She joined VIWU in 1990.

Sandy Shreve was raised in Sackville, New Brunswick, and moved to Vancouver in 1971. An office worker for the past 15 years, Shreve now works as the Departmental Assistant in Women's Studies at SFU. Her poems have been published in a variety of journals and anthologies. Her first book of poetry, *The Speed of the Wheel is Up to the Potter*, was published by Quarry Press in 1990. She was the guest editor of *Working For A Living*, a special issue of the feminist journal *Room of One's Own* (1988) which features stories and poems by women about their work. Sandy first joined VIWU in 1980, and was a more or less casual member for a year or so. She has been with the group on a regular basis since 1985.

Pam Tranfield was born in 1960 in Nanaimo, British Columbia. She has been a member of VIWU since 1985. Her work has appeared in a number of publications including *event, Room of One's Own, Fireweed, Other Voices, Prairie Journal*, and *NeWest Review* and in the anthology *East of Main* (Pulp Press, edited by Tom Wayman and Calvin Wharton). She now works full-time as a mother, and part-time in the order department of a natural foods wholesale company.

M.C. Warrior alternates between working as a househusband and a cook/deckhand on fish boats. He is also a member of the General Executive Board of the United Fishermen and Allied Workers' Union. He has previously appeared in several anthologies and has had one book published, *Quitting Time* (McLeod Books, 1978). He is a founding member of VIWU.

Tom Wayman, born 1945, remains a VIWU member although he is now the Squire of "Appledore," an estate tucked into the Selkirk Mountains near Nelson, in B.C.'s southeast. When he isn't running his estate, he teaches writing at the Kelowna campus of Okanagan College. Wayman's most recent books include *In a Small House on the Outskirts of Heaven*, a collection of his poems, from Harbour Publishing in 1989, and *East of Main: An Anthology of Poems from East Vancouver*, co-edited with Calvin Wharton, from Pulp Press, 1989.

ACKNOWLEDGEMENTS:
Some of the material in *More than Our Jobs* has appeared previously in the following: *Arc, Canadian Jewish Outlook, Canadian Dimension, CPPNW Quarterly* (Canadian Physicians for the Prevention of Nuclear War), *Don't Quit Yr Day-Job, East of Main* (Pulp Press), *event, Fireweed, The Fisherman, The Guardian* (Hospital Employees Union), *Labour/Le Travail, The Malahat Review, The Naked Physician* (Quarry Press), *New Directions, New Voices* (Mosaic Press), *Ontario Review, Other Voices, Paper Bag Poems, Paper Work* (Harbour Publishing), *Poetry Northwest, Prism international, Room of One's Own, Saturday Night, Tradeswoman, Westcoast Mariner*.

"(guide to executive suicide)" and accompanying sketch used with permission from *Amanuensis* by Phil Hall (Brick Books)

"Labour Pantoum" and "Mrs. Copp" used with permission from *Are We There Yet?* by Kirsten Emmott (Pierian Press)

"Skywriting" used with permission from *An X-Ray of Longing* by Glen Downie (Polestar Press)

"Laid Off," "Abortion," "Taking Back the Night," and "White Lies" used with permission from *The Speed of the Wheel Is Up to the Potter* by Sandy Shreve (Quarry Press)

"Only Movement of Your Needle," "Allegiances," "Song of the Second Mouth," "Poison on the Wind," and "Incantation to Change Our Lives" used with permission from *Colour of Winter Air* by Zoë Landale (Sono Nis Press)